NEW DIRECTIONS
in
CELLO PLAYING

How to make cello playing
easier and
play without pain

VICTOR SAZER

Foreword by
PAUL KATZ

Library of Congress Catalog Card Number: 94-092427

ISBN: 0-944810-02-0

Editor: Nina Sazer O'Donnell

Line Drawings: Lea Lam Knight

Cover Art and Design: Tony Gleason

Photographs: 5,7,8,11,12,14,15: Margery Fain
Photographs: 1,2,3,4,6,9,10,13,16,17: Patty Lemke

Reproduction page 75: Dimitry Markevitch
Reproduction page 74: National Gallery of Victoria, Australia
Reproduction page 55: Richard Norris, M.D.
Reproduced material pages 88 and 89: American String Teachers Association

Published by: *ofnote*
Post Office Box 66760
Los Angeles, CA 90066 U.S.A.

Printed in the United States of America

Dedicated to Betty
She sang of Peace
and Justice
and Love
and
Universal Brotherhood

Acknowledgments

Special thanks are due to Nina Sazer O'Donnell for her superb editing. As a writer and editor who also plays the cello, she was able to test both the concepts and the language of this book.

Thanks also to Lea Lam Knight for her lovely drawings, Tony Gleason for his cover art, Margery Fain and Patty Lemke for their photographs and Nancy Stein for her French-English translation.

I am grateful to Elizabeth Morrison for assisting in initiating this project and to Margery Fain, Willy Krebbers, Elizabeth Morrison, Richard McNalley, Lenore Sazer-Krebbers, Marc Sazer and Leon Vallens for their invaluable proofreading.

Marc Sazer, who is applying the approach of this book to violin playing, was extremely helpful with his astute observations throughout the writing process.

I will always appreciate Pam Hartman, teacher of the Alexander Technique and Physio-Synthesis, for teaching this sloucher to enjoy standing up straight and balanced.

And finally, I would like to thank to Paul Katz for his generous foreword and Dr. Richard Norris for his kind words and pre-publication review.

V.S.

Foreword

This is quite an extraordinary book—certainly one of the best books on basic body mechanics ever written for the cello. That's a big statement which I make not only out of enthusiasm but carefully, and with a real sense of responsibility. I want cellists to read, study and use this book because it has the potential to improve playing and alleviate a lot of pain and suffering.

I have always been wary of the dangers involved in attempting to change bow arms, hand positions and other techniques using self-study of the printed word. In reading the manuscript of *New Directions in Cello Playing,* however, I was relieved to find that the majority of what is written here felt really safe. How could any reader possibly get into trouble with an approach which promotes the player's self-awareness of body balance, position and tension free movements. This may be a dangerous assumption, however, because someone can always find a way to misinterpret and misapply.

In writing this foreword then, I want to impress upon readers how critical it is to approach Mr. Sazer's ideas, some of which are authentically new to the cello world, not only with openness, but with thoughtfulness and intelligence. I admire Vic Sazer's clarity and logical evolution of thought. Yet on a subject as complex as how body parts move, balance each other and inter-relate, misunderstanding is still possible.

One does not have to agree with every page or every thought to profit from this book. There are a number of points that don't speak to me. This does not, however, diminish my enthusiasm for what I find to be so many wonderful perceptions. And I have such respect for Vic Sazer that I will continue to think about and experiment with everything he says.

The key to successfully using this book for self-study lies in one's ability to tune in on their own body. Those who have some experience in a discipline other than the cello such as Yoga, Tai Chi, or Meditation, may have already developed a greater sense of what is tight, what is loose or what is free-breathing. When performing the exercises in this book, look for tension or immobility of which you might be unaware.

Self-awareness cannot be assumed. A young cellist who recently came to play for me attacked the Dvorak Concerto with a death-grip bow arm, joints locked, thumb squeezing and with his finger nails purple and white from forcing. I began my discussion of his performance by telling him that we needed to address his excessive tension and asked him to describe any fatigue or soreness. "What? I have no problem! My arm never gets so tired that I can't play. My thumb gets weak and my arm gets numb, but you don't have to worry—I just have to build more strength." If that statement makes any sense to you, consider it again after you've read this book.

There are many people playing with unrecognized and debilitating levels of muscular tension, who like the boy who played Dvorak, are so accustomed to this tension that it feels normal. Some consider physical pain a necessary evil to be endured in order to have the energy and strength to play. In our everyday lives we have been taught to push our body to the limit by doing more sit-ups, lifting more weights and running to exhaustion in order to gain strength and endurance. It's sometimes hard, therefore, to convince people that this is not the best way to play the cello.

It is far better for cellists to learn from the martial arts of the Far East which focus on balancing the body, loosening joints, relaxing muscles, using body weight rather than flexed muscles for strength and breathing in ways that promote balance and ease. Motion functions naturally when unimpaired and brings agility, vibrancy and power (explosive if needed) to any activity.

Of course, Western athletes demonstrate the same principles. Imagine a football running back who is loose enough to dart, turn, twist, change directions, throw or catch a ball and still run straight through 300 pounds of opposing beef. It's easy to see that there are no tightly flexed muscles, no rigid joints and that a stiff leg, wrist or neck would inhibit body motion and make all of this impossible. How many of us have achieved that degree of looseness, balance, ease of motion and strength?

When this running back reaches to the right to catch a ball his leg will move to the left. Before jumping high in the air, his knees bend in a preparatory motion opposite to the direction of the jump. The interaction of the body is a complex but natural mechanism which gives athletes and cellists optimum agility and strength when not blocked by rigidity.

Mr. Sazer's wonderful demonstrations show how to apply such universal principles of motion and body mechanics to playing the cello. In particular, his suggestions for how to find a healthy seated position and how to use the feet to steer the body are truly exciting. These ideas, which are new to me, have given me an increased sense of buoyancy and freedom of movement.

One of the world's most remarkable cellists, Janos Starker, recently told me he could best describe his entire lifetime of cello playing as the continual discovery and release of smaller and smaller points of muscular tension. We should all follow his example and I believe that this book can be an important part of the process of self-discovery that leads us in that direction.

Paul Katz
Cleveland Quartet
Professor of Cello
Eastman School of Music

Introduction

My cello studies were guided by several fine teachers and I learned a great deal from each of them. Yet I am perhaps most grateful to my first teacher, Charles Brennand Sr., for advice he gave me during my very first lesson.

Before he let me touch my cello, he held up a pencil, explaining that musicians sometimes need to write fingerings and bowings in their music, "but only in pencil. Never in ink! You never know when you'll get a better idea. And furthermore, always look for one." Years later I realized that he taught his students much more than music and cello playing. He taught us to think for ourselves and be open to change.

I recall periods of disorientation during my student days, when a change from one teacher to another required that I adjust to a new method or school of playing. Each teacher seemed to have different notions about cello playing and their instructions were often contradictory.

> Hold your cello high–low–turned one way or another–keep your hand parallel to the fingerboard–at this angle or that. Your fingers are little hammers–don't hammer your fingers–press lightly–firmly–don't press– hang your arm on the string–sink your fingers into the fingerboard–rest your arm weight on your bow–use gravity–balance–hold your bow firmly–lightly–increase pressure as you go toward the point–with your first finger–your hand–arm–back or not at all. *And above all*, RELAX!

At some point I began to wonder if there were objective criteria or principles which defined the best way of doing things, or if there was a best way at all. I also wondered why some cellists play with comfort and ease while others struggle like Don Quixote in mortal combat with windmills.

When I learned about the high incidence of performance-related injury among cellists I had more questions. Why do so many who play this glorious instrument live with pain and discomfort as their constant companions? Can pain be prevented or is it unavoidable?

Curiosity and an incorrigible bent for experimentation keeps me grappling with these and other questions about cello playing. This life-long quest for answers has been important to me both as a cellist and as a teacher.

Key Principles

Over time, I learned that there are indeed underlying principles which can guide cellists toward more effortless and pain-free playing. They are neither secrets nor the property of any one school of playing. Nor are they solely applicable to playing the cello.

They are observable principles of body movement which govern all human activity from ordinary to complex. Anyone can apply these principles. It only requires increasing awareness of the body's natural impulses and removing the roadblocks that get in their way. *The key is awareness. The goal is to allow the body to do what comes naturally.*

By studying and applying these principles, I found some alternatives to standard cello techniques which make playing easier and alleviate pain. I would like to share what I have learned with others who are hooked on playing the cello.

About This Book

This book address musicians' pain problems in general, including the causes of pain, types of injuries and pain prevention. It introduces natural, tension-free ways to play the cello. It presents anatomically-improved ways of sitting and holding the cello, a new approach to left arm and hand techniques and fundamentals of bowing. It also discusses other familiar but often-neglected elements of cello technique.

Readers are guided through a process of self-discovery designed to increase awareness of the body's natural impulses. Hands-on demonstrations are included, to enable readers to compare their experiences with the author's observations.

Contents

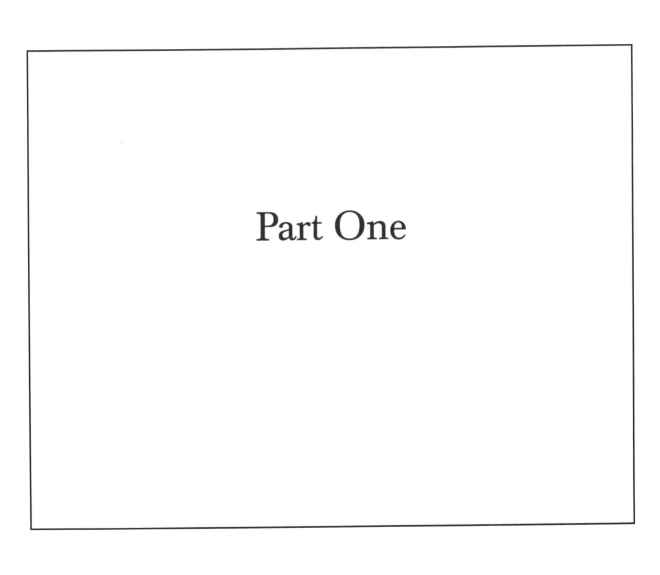

Part One

Chapter One
Musicians and Pain

Rates of Pain and Injury

Would you guess that most musicians experience pain from playing their instruments? Would you guess that they have more injuries than football players? Astounding as this may seem, it is true. Health Magazine reported that 65 percent of professional football players suffered serious career-related injuries compared to 75 percent of professional musicians.[1] Although playing the cello is not a contact sport and broken bones are not typical, other serious physical problems are common among cellists.

A 1987 study of more than 2,000 musicians in 47 professional orchestras found that 76 percent of musicians reported at least one medical problem severe enough to affect their performance. The study also found that medical problems are most prevalent among string players.[2]

---

[1] *Health Magazine,* May/June 1993.
[2] International Conference of Symphony and Opera Musicians, *Senza Sordino,* August 1987.

Pain Affects All Musicians

Pain problems are not new to musicians. Numerous written accounts of performance-related pain among musicians can be found in medical literature dating back to the early 1800s. The time is long overdue to give serious attention to identifying and alleviating musicians' pain.

Pain does not respect musical accomplishment. Cellists in all fields and at all levels suffer pain and injury, including celebrated artists, students, soloists, orchestral and chamber players, studio musicians and amateurs. Among all musicians, cellists are known for having the highest frequency of back problems.

Musicians have been understandably reluctant to acknowledge performance-related pain. Many fear that doing so will jeopardize their public image or livelihood. Players still hesitate to acknowledge the source of their performance-related disabilities, although more information about the treatment of physical injuries is available now than ever before.

Conditioning to Accept Pain

There is considerable evidence that conditioning musicians to accept pain begins at an early age. Pressure to achieve often leads to a *no pain, no gain* approach to instrumental study. Such pressure encourages lifelong patterns of accepting pain as normal. A 1988 study of advanced secondary school music students in Houston, Texas, found that nearly 80 percent of the students considered pain acceptable for achieving technique.[3]

---

[3] Lockwood A., Medical Problems in Secondary School-Aged Musicians. *Medical Problems of Performing Artists*, December 1988.

The same study also found a higher rate of injury among cellists and bass players than other instrumentalists.

Today it is common for music schools to provide in-house physical therapy services or use nearby medical centers to treat students' pain problems. In 1992 the Juilliard School of Music established an on-campus staff of three physical therapists to treat performance-related injuries.

Music Medicine and Ergonomics

Recent studies of musicians' physical problems are stimulating new interest and research. Music Medicine and Performing Arts Medicine have emerged as new medical specialties. Research and treatment centers for performing artists are being established in many areas. More journals, books and articles are available on this subject than ever before.

Ergonomics is a newly-evolving science which addresses the physical problems of workers in many fields. It is the study of how to adapt work environments and equipment to the physical needs of workers, based on how the human body works. Developments in this field also provide guidance for addressing the physical problems of musicians.

"If a muscle doesn't make music, don't use it."
—*Emanuel Feuermann*

Chapter Two
Causes of Pain

Is pain inevitable? Is it the price one must pay in order to play?

Many cellists believe that pain cannot be avoided. Finding no physical relief from their performance-related pain, they are convinced that their art requires the sacrifice of their bodies. There are also many who believe that what is good for the body and the physical requirements of playing the cello represent an unresolvable dichotomy.

The Seeds of Pain

The seeds of pain are most often sown during our earliest lessons. Fledgling cellists too often learn techniques which conflict with the natural laws of body motion. With practice, these unnatural playing patterns become deeply ingrained.

Over time, unnatural movements are likely to cause pain. Some fortunate cellists avoid this pitfall by intuitively finding ways of using their bodies more naturally.

While explaining the importance of careful practice to Mikey, a bright ten-year-old student, I pointed out that one learns from *all* practice: "If you practice something right, you learn it right. If you practice it wrong, you learn it that way, too." Almost before I finished my sentence he interjected, "You mean that practice doesn't make perfect; *practice makes permanent.*"

Overuse and Repetitive Motions

Some experts attribute pain entirely to overuse. Overuse injuries occur when body tissues are stressed by repeatedly pushing them beyond their limits. Although overuse always requires careful attention, it is only one of many causes of pain for musicians. Focusing solely on overuse without probing the specifics of body use and instrumental methodology is of limited practical value to cellists.

Repetitive motions can certainly lead to pain. Yet all repetitive motions do not result in pain. The frequency, force and manner in which they are performed can vary considerably, as can their effects.

When repetitive motions generate a great deal of tension they cause pain. The effects are different, however, when repetitive motions create little or no tension.

Try the following to test different types of repetitive motions.

Step 1. Snap your forearm vigorously from side to side until you feel tension or fatigue. Stop and rest when you feel discomfort.

Step 2. Move your forearm in an oval-shaped path.

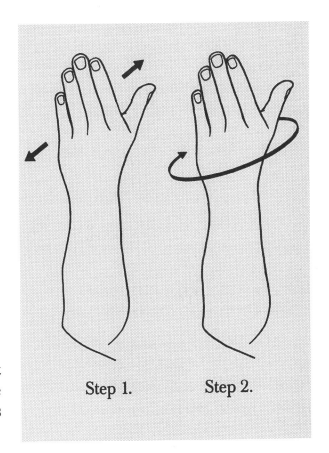

Step 1.   Step 2.

Did changing the path of movement reduce tension and increase endurance?

Observation
This example shows that even a slight alteration in the path of a repetitive motion can make a big difference in its physical effect.

Improper Body Use

The basic causes of pain and injury have more to do with how you use your body than with how frequently you perform various motions. Improper body use is the primary cause of pain. Improper body use also increases the risk of overuse injuries. Yet playing in pain is not inevitable.

Most pain is related to poor body balance. Faulty alignment, immobility and pressing are the major causes of imbalance. Body imbalance creates muscle tension which often accumulates layer upon layer. This prevents the body from functioning freely and can cause a variety of serious and painful problems.

Improper body use, the root cause of pain, is like having a pebble in your shoe. Unattended, it can go on and on as a nagging discomfort. Or it can cause increasingly severe damage over time.

Types of Tension

All body movement involves functional tension. Functional tension occurs when muscles contract and lengthen to move the body or any of its parts. One does not feel this kind of tension, however. It is not excessive and causes no pain.

Tension beyond this functional level is excessive and counter productive. It can be physically damaging as well as musically limiting. Excessive tension anywhere in the body diminishes endurance and significantly increases the danger of injury. The term *tension* will be used in this book to describe excessive tension, or tension which inhibits rather than creates motion.

Chapter Three
Types of Injuries

The most common injuries among musicians involve joints, muscles, nerves, tendons and the back.

Joints

Joints are the body's hinges and shock absorbers. They are most frequently injured when they are misaligned or forced to move beyond their normal range of motion. Joints can also be injured by excessive pressing or by jolting movements.

Muscles

Muscles are elastic fibers which contract and lengthen to move the body and all of its parts. Muscles are arranged in opposing groups. Motion occurs when one group of muscles contracts while its opposing group lengthens.

Excessive tension can prevent a muscle group that should be lengthening from doing so. This happens when opposing muscles contract at the same time. When used improperly, muscles and connected tendons can become inflamed or torn. When muscles are repeatedly torn, scar tissue replaces normal muscle fiber. Even when this damage occurs in tiny increments, its cumulative effect can permanently limit flexibility.

> "... injuries may worsen over time: scar tissue slowly replaces muscle. The scar tissue can impede surrounding muscles, leading to more microtears and more scar tissue. Eventually, scar tissue dominates."
>
> *—Emil Pascarelli, M.D.*

Nerves

Nerves are cord-like bundles of fibers made up of axons. They form a network of pathways which carries information to and from the brain and other parts of the body. Nerve injury usually results from nerve compression or entrapment. The most frequent and well-known injury of this kind is Carpal Tunnel Syndrome.

Carpal Tunnel Syndrome (CTS)

Tendons and the median nerve pass through the carpal tunnel in the wrist which has limited space. Rapid finger movements combined with an excessively bent wrist can irritate and inflame the tendons.

This causes the tendons to swell. Swelling diminishes the space within the carpal tunnel and compresses the median nerve, disrupting communication between the hand and the brain. The result can be pain, numbness, tingling or weakening of the thumb and the first and middle fingers.

This occupational injury is responsible for about half of all current work-related injuries in the United States. CTS is widespread among those who work at computer keyboards for long periods and others who regularly move their fingers rapidly while their wrists bend downward.

Using a similar arm and hand position to perform rapid finger movements can likewise cause CTS for cellists. Although keeping the wrist excessively high while performing rapid finger movements can induce CTS, researchers at Pennsylvania State University have recently found that a lowered wrist (wrist extension) is more dangerous than a raised wrist (wrist flexion).[4]

---

[4] *Los Angeles Times,* September 28, 1994.

Tendons

Tendons are fibrous tissues which connect muscles to bones. Trauma and strain can inflame or tear tendons, causing painful tendinitis. Frequently re-injuring tendons stimulates the formation of calcium deposits. When these deposits become extensive they must be surgically removed. Tendon damage can be one of the most debilitating injuries.

Although the dictionary defines tendinitis as the inflammation of a tendon, this term is commonly used to refer to trauma of muscles, tendons, a combination of muscles and tendons or the musculo-tendinous unit.

The Back

The back is a complex support system for the body. A key component of the back is the spine, which consists of 33 stacked bones, or vertebrae. The upper 24 of these bones are separated by gel-filled cushioning discs.

The back also contains the spinal cord, which includes a cable of nerves that transmits impulses to and from the brain, controlling all activities below the neck; 31 pairs of nerves from the spinal cord which transmit information between the brain and the muscles; approximately 400 muscles; and about 1,000 tendons.

Cellists commonly injure their backs by using techniques which compress or twist the spine. This can rupture spinal discs and stress back muscles and tendons. Sitting positions which keep the body off balance are a major cause of back pain.

Chapter Four
Preventing Pain

Avoiding Injury

Many harmful effects of improper body use can be prevented by learning to play without tension. This requires that we first learn to identify the sources of tension.

Everyone knows that physical limitations are real. Some believe, however, that playing the cello demands exceeding these limits. Yet pushing beyond realistic limits inevitably leads to pain.

Wise musicians take responsibility for protecting their bodies by refusing to allow circumstances to push them beyond safe limits.

While the most important defense against performance-related injuries is to learn to play in ways which do not cause pain, musicians can also develop protective strategies. For example, when orchestral players are required to perform extended stressful passages, they can prevent injuries by alternately resting or easing up. The varying of fingerings and bowings can also reduce stress.

Concern for the physical well-being of musicians must be a high priority for conductors and orchestra managers as well playing musicians. Given the disproportionately high injury rate, awareness and education are needed for all concerned.

Physical Conditioning

Keeping physically fit through regular exercise is as important for musicians as for athletes. Programs such as the Alexander Technique, Tai Chi or Yoga can help musicians to align and balance their bodies. Many music schools now have Alexander Technique instructors on staff. Tai Chi is practiced by more people, worldwide, than any other body-conditioning program and Yoga has been used for physical and mental development for about six thousand years.

Any conditioning program that teaches you how to balance your body, breathe freely and expand your spine and joints can be helpful. Such programs promote good health, stimulate a sense of well-being and can significantly reduce performance anxiety, as well as tension. When engaging in such activities, however, be sure to avoid exercises that are not comfortable. A good rule of thumb is to trust your own body and never do anything that hurts.

It is important to keep your body balanced and mobile. Avoid pressing or forcing and never play through pain. Sufficient rest time during playing sessions is also essential. Systematically stretching and warming up before playing can protect your body and make it less injury-prone. Cold muscles are more vulnerable to injury because they are less pliable.

It is best to avoid high-impact or jolting movements in daily activities, exercise and when playing the cello. These movements cause the body to automatically react by vigorously contracting the muscles to protect them from further injury. Such contractions can cause pain and injuries.

Balance and Alignment

The marvelous structural engineering of the human body must be protected and well-maintained to function efficiently. Like a well-constructed building, it must have a strong frame and a solid foundation. Your body's skeletal frame and muscles must be balanced to be strong, and your feet must be properly placed to provide a stable and supportive foundation.

If a building has a defective foundation or is out of alignment, it is weak and unsafe. If your body is misaligned, however, it adjusts to protect its weakened frame. It does this by lengthening some muscles and shortening others. This does not eliminate the basic imbalance. It is simply how the body compensates to protect itself from further injury.

If a basic imbalance is not corrected, this adaptive process continues, causing some muscles to become stronger while others weaken. Over time, imbalance and flawed alignment become accepted as normal.

Combining a good physical conditioning program with improved playing methods can improve muscle balance and correct misalignments. With proper training or re-training, the body's innate adaptive capability can restore healthy body alignment.

Those who guide young musicians during their formative years bear a very special responsibility. They are the ones who can best prepare their students for a lifetime of pain-free playing. While many teachers and music schools are aware of pain problems, pain-free playing methods and physical conditioning programs designed specifically for musicians need wider attention and development.

> "Music schools are failing us, because they don't stress physical conditioning. Most musicians fail to grasp that they are athletes. . . . "
> *—Emil Pascarelli, M.D.*

Natural Playing

Most motions used to play the cello are natural and familiar to our bodies. They are instinctive and we use them daily. Learning to play the cello does not require us to learn new motions, but to apply motions our bodies already know to a new activity.

Most of us can lift our arms and let them fall. We can pick things up and put them down, wiggle our fingers and pull or move our arms in many directions. These are all motions we use for cello playing as well as for a myriad of other activities. Seemingly complex motions are usually combinations of simple ones, just as complicated words are combinations of simple syllables.

Observing how we use our bodies in everyday activities can provide insight into the nature of body movement. Just by being alive, we perform an amazing variety of intricate motions without a second thought. Babies do not have to be taught how to crawl or to walk. When their bodies are ready they intuitively do what comes naturally.

The principles of body movement are the same when we walk, play the cello, perform brain surgery or chop onions.

Our greatest challenge in learning to play the cello is to build on our instinctive impulses rather than to obstruct them.

"It is not stressed often enough that the playing of an instrument is physical work and therefore the same rules can be applied to it as to any other activity in which skill is demanded. A certain amount of timidity leads musicians to fear that they will be considered craftsmen, not artists, if they give importance to the physical aspects of playing."[5]
—*Emanuel Feuermann*

[5] Itzkoff, S.W., *Emanuel Feuermann, Virtuoso*. University of Alabama Press, 1979.

Although most motions used to play the cello are natural, knowing how to play the cello is not. Specialized skills must be learned and aspiring cellists must go to a teacher for instruction. This is often a critical formative event. Will the teacher encourage the use of natural body motions or inadvertently construct obstacles which subvert them?

Learning to Play the Cello

Learning to play the cello is like learning any other skill. Known motions are merged in new combinations and transformed into a specialized new vocabulary. For cellists, this is largely a tactile vocabulary–a cello vocabulary. As this vocabulary develops, we make connections between new sensations and those we already know from past experience and intuition. This process is similar to learning to swim. Familiar body, arm and leg movements form a new tactile vocabulary to meet the physical requirements of this activity.

Musicians Are Athletes

Musicians have a great deal in common with athletes. Both engage in activities demanding high levels of physical efficiency, balance and grace. They each strive to perform their most challenging feats with the greatest of ease.

> "Musicians are, in fact highly specialized athletes . . ."[6]
> —*Jack S. Winberg, M.D. and Merle F. Salus, M.S.T.*

[6] Winberg, J.S., Salus, M.F., *Stretching for Strings*. ASTA, College Town Press, Bloomington, 1990.

Preventing Pain

How can we prevent injury and pain? How do we develop pain-free cello techniques? Although some pain problems are complicated and may require considerable training or retraining, many are simple and easily correctable.

The first step is to increase awareness and understanding of our bodies and how they work. Our bodies continually provide us with information. Yet we too often ignore or do not understand their messages. Awareness is the first step.

The second step is to re-evaluate our basic assumptions about cello playing. Because no school of cello playing is immune to pain or injury, the path to progress must include a careful re-examination of all widely used practices.

This evaluation need not be overwhelming or complicated. It does not require an advanced degree or special equipment. To succeed, a cellist must only be alive and able to breathe and feel. As you will see, your own body is your best guide to more natural and tension-free playing. Each one of us is a living laboratory equipped with all of the diagnostic equipment needed for this process.

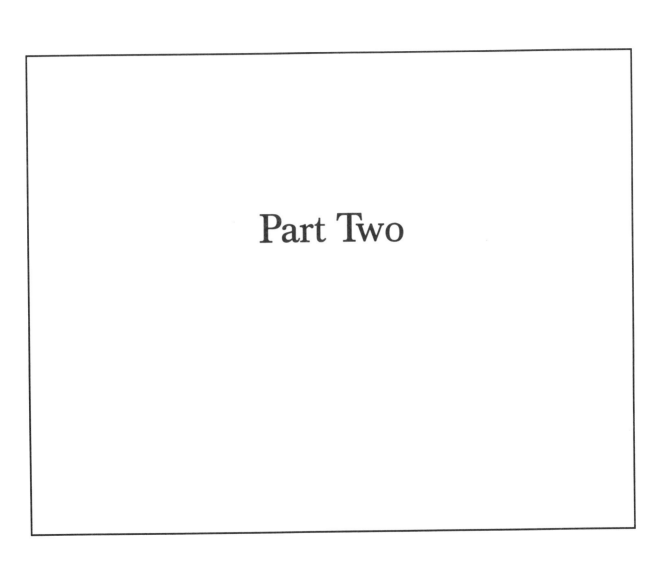

Part Two

Chapter Five
Getting Acquainted With Your Body

About the Demonstrations

The best way to become better acquainted with your body and increase your understanding of how it works is to observe how it feels to perform particular actions.

From this point forward, demonstrations are suggested to enable you to physically experience the concepts presented. They will help you to identify sources of physical tension and discover tension-free methods of playing.

Some demonstrations are performed without the cello. These will help you explore basic principles of body movement. Others illustrate body motions which are similar to those used in cello playing. Demonstrations with the cello are also included.

Perform these demonstrations as experiments in your own process of self-discovery. Increasing awareness of how you use your body can free you from unwanted tension.

Observe your reactions to each demonstration and consider how they relate to your cello playing. Evaluate the demonstrations for yourself first. Then compare your results with the author's observations which follow most of the demonstrations.

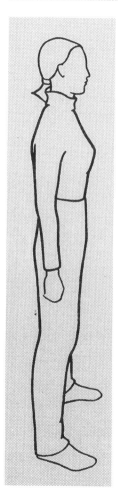

Balanced Stance

Several of the demonstrations ask you to assume a *balanced stance*. Find this body alignment in the following way:

1. Stand tall with your feet about shoulder width or a little farther apart.

2. Let the crown of your head face the ceiling and expand your lungs.

3. With your sternum up, release your shoulders and tuck your pelvis under.

4. Bend your knees slightly—just enough to make sure that they are not locked.

5. Balance your weight on the ball and heel of each foot.

Do not rest on the outer edges of your feet. This rotates your hips to a position which weakens support for your back, whether you are standing or sitting. Turn your feet toward your little toes to test the difference.

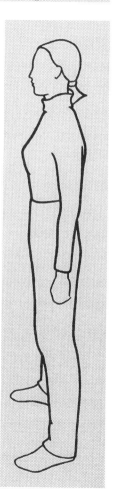

Identifying Sources of Tension

Muscle tension is a major cause of pain and injury. To eliminate this tension, you must first be able to identify its sources. The demonstrations in this chapter are designed to heighten your awareness of the sources of tension.

The Breath Test

The breath test is our most important diagnostic tool. It is both the simplest and most effective way to tell if our bodies are tension-free or not.

When our bodies are completely balanced, we are tension-free and able to breathe deeply and completely. Our bodies are at their peak of efficiency in this state. When tension is present our breathing is immediately restricted. This information helps us to discover where the tension resides.

In many ways, the breath test is our best teacher. It is an unfailing tension detector and sends clear signals to guide us to the most tension-free ways of using our bodies.

Demonstration 1

The Breath Test

Breathe deeply as you perform each of the following steps.

Step 1. Assume a balanced stance.

Step 2. Lean your head forward.

Step 3. Lean your head to one side.

Step 4. Turn your torso a degree or two to one side.

Step 5. Rotate your torso gently from side to side with even, continuous motion.

Step 6. Lean your torso slightly forward.

Step 7. Hold your elbow a bit behind your back.

Step 8. Lift one or both of your shoulders.

Step 9. Pull one or both of your shoulders forward.

Step 10. Bend your wrists downward.

Step 11. Experiment with other body positions.

Is your breathing restricted in some positions?

Can you breathe more freely in some positions than in others?

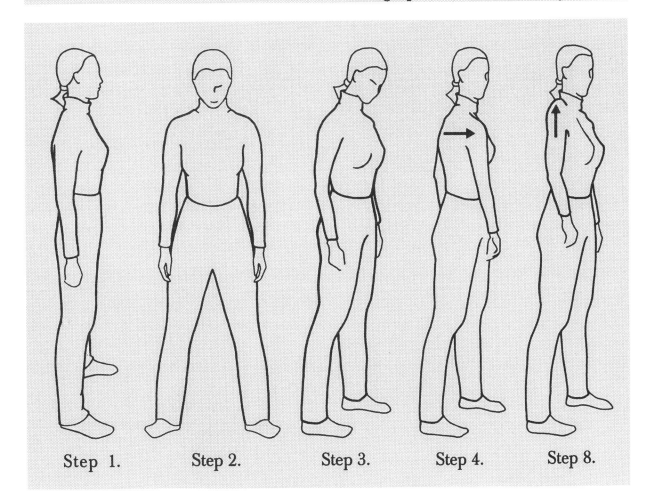

Step 1.   Step 2.   Step 3.   Step 4.   Step 8.

Observations

Tension is created when your body is out of balance. When your body is well balanced in steps one and five you are able to breathe deeply and freely. In step five the continuous symmetrical rotating keeps your body balanced. Tension occurs, however, when your torso stays turned to one side, even for a short time.

In all of the other steps, tension is created because your body is out of balance. This is confirmed by your restricted breathing.

Consider how this affects cellists who routinely lean forward, pull one or both shoulders up or move their shoulders forward when they play. What about those who keep their bodies or heads turned to one side or play with their heads down?

Some cellists always turn their bodies to the left to play on the A string. Some bring their right arms behind their backs to play on the C string. Many cellists lean forward continually or when they play in the upper registers. They may be unaware that these alignments create tension, make playing more difficult and increase the risk of pain.

The breath test is our litmus test.

Demonstration 2

Alignment and Balance

This demonstration helps explore how body alignment and balance affect muscle tension.

Step 1. Tilt your head slightly forward. Let go, releasing all of the muscles in your torso and allowing your upper body to fall forward.

Step 2. Lean your torso a bit forward. Let go.

Step 3. Raise one shoulder. Let go.

Step 4. Twist your torso to one side. Let go.

Step 5. Rotate your torso symmetrically from side to side. Let go.

Step 6. Assume a balanced stance. Let go.

Does your upper body fall forward when you let go in some of the steps?

Does your upper body fall to one side when you let go in some of the steps?

Does your body remain erect in any of the steps?

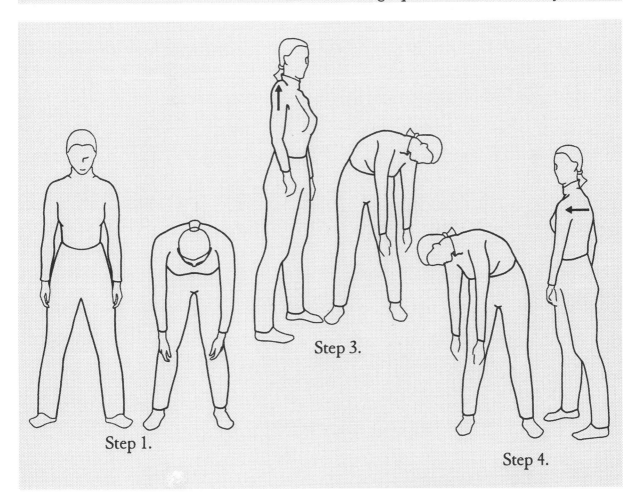

Step 1.

Step 3.

Step 4.

Observations

When you let go in steps one through four, your upper body falls forward or to one side. When you let go in steps five and six your body remains erect. Why?

In each of the first four steps, your body is off balance. When you lean your head (which weighs several pounds) forward, extra weight is shifted so that it is in front of your center of gravity. This is why your torso falls forward when you let go. When you twist your body, tilt your head or raise your shoulder, extra weight is again shifted, causing you to be off-balance. This makes you fall to one side when you release.

On the other hand, when you let go in well-balanced positions, such as in steps five and six, your body remains comfortably erect. In step five, you maintain good balance by symmetrically turning your body from side to side. Keeping your torso turned and immobile, even for a short time in step four, however, undermines your balance.

Whenever your body is off balance, your muscles are forced to do extra work to keep your body upright. This extra work causes tension which can lead to discomfort or pain.

Chapter Six
Gravity, Balance and Body Use

Gravity

Gravity is a constant downward force. If permitted, it pulls your head down toward your neck and your trunk down toward your hips. It also compresses or rounds your spine and makes your body sag. You can cope with gravity by either actively lifting or passively submitting to it.

You cannot submit completely, of course, because just being alive requires lifting. You can, however, give in enough to significantly reduce your body's efficiency and increase your risk of injury. When your body is lifted and well balanced, your spine and joints expand and you are able to breathe without restriction. With this body alignment, gravity becomes an asset rather than a liability.

> Columbia astronauts Richard Hieb and Dr. Chiaki Mukai measured each other's spine with an ultrasound imaging machine during their July 1994 space flight. They found, that like all astronauts in outer space, they had grown a few inches because the spine stretches at zero gravity.[7]

It may seem at first glance that lifting or extending your body upward requires more effort than allowing it to relax downward. This is not the case, however. In fact, the greatest freedom of movement can only be achieved when you are lifting your body.

Although total relaxation may be appropriate for resting or meditation, it is hardly the condition to be in when you are playing your cello. To play the cello, you must be free of tension, but also alert, balanced and poised for action.

Body Use and Walking

Most cellists use their bodies in one of these three ways when they play: they either apply downward pressure, release body weight downward, or lift their bodies. Although many combine these approaches, it is useful to explore the characteristics of each.

The next demonstration illustrates three distinct ways that people use their bodies. The distinctions are observable in all activities, including walking and cello playing.

[7] *Associated Press,* July 20, 1994.

Demonstration 3

Three Ways of Walking

Perform the breath test with each step.

Step 1. Walk, pressing your feet downward against the ground.

Step 2. Walk, relaxing your body weight downward.

Step 3. Walk, maintaining a balanced stance. Focus on lifting your body. Be sure that you pivot from the heel to the ball of each foot.

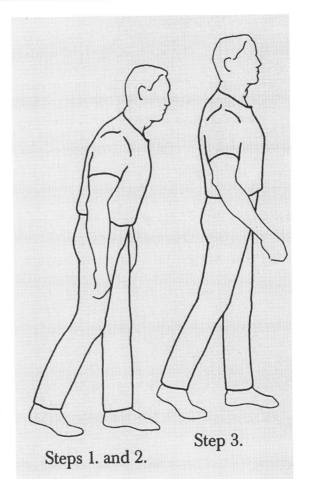

Steps 1. and 2. Step 3.

Which way of walking feels best?

Which way gives you the greatest feeling of strength, buoyancy and well-being?

Which way allows you to breathe most freely?

Observations

Notice that when you press your feet against the ground or relax your body downward, your body feels heavy and your trunk tends to lean forward. Walking in either of these ways restricts your breathing. In contrast, your trunk remains erect when you lift your body. You feel more energetic, light on your feet and you are able to breathe freely.

"In the living body not even sleep can bring the centre of gravity to a perfect standstill, and moving about will make it swing considerably."[8]

—*Otto Szendy and Mihaly Nemessuri*

Balance

Like a scale, the human body always seeks balance. When you depress one side of a scale, the other side rises. When you release it, the scale see-saws until equilibrium is re-established.

Unlike a scale, however, the human body is *always* in motion. Its center of gravity is constantly shifting in a series of continuous counter-balancing reactions. The body is like a flexible combination of several scales. It can balance its parts even when they move in different directions and on different planes.

Allowing this balancing process to function freely is a fundamental key to playing the cello more easily and alleviating pain.

[8] Szedy, O., Nemessuri, M., *The Physiology of Violin Playing*, Akademiai Kiado, Budapest, 1971.

Opposites

Opposites are implicit to the concept of balance. Physics teaches that every action has an equal and opposite reaction. If one part of your body moves without a counter-balancing motion in the opposite direction, your body is off balance and tension is created.

Because your center of gravity is always in motion, counterbalancing movements are also constant. Since your body is so much heavier than your arm, a relatively small body movement or impulse can propel your arm a greater distance than the motion of your body. Often, the body impulse is so slight that it is not even visible. It may only be felt as resistance to an arm movement in the opposite direction.

When your bow arm and your body move in opposite directions at the same time, the friction created between the bow and string enables you to produce a sound easily. If, however, your bow arm and body move in the same direction at the same time, this friction is partially or completely neutralized. It then takes greater force to produce sound.

There are many observable instances of opposites balancing one another. When you walk, your arms move in the opposite direction from your legs to keep your body balanced. When you move your arm up and down to wave, your hand moves in the opposite direction from your arm.

> When Daniel, my nine-year-old grandson, asked for help opening a tight cabinet door, I suggested that he move his body toward the door as he pulls the knob away from it. To his delight, the troublesome door opened immediately.

Demonstration 4

Balance in Motion

This demonstration illustrates how movement affects body balance.

Step 1. Assume a balanced stance.

Step 2. Draw large and small circles in the air in front of you with your right arm. Allow your body to move as it is naturally inclined to do.

Step 4. Draw spirals, figure eights and other shapes of varying sizes. Notice how your body moves. Be aware of the sensations in your feet.

Step 5. Draw circles or other shapes but do not allow your body to move.

Step 6. Draw circles or other shapes. Initiate your movements by steering your body with your feet. Allow your arm to react to the movements of your body.

Step 7. Experiment with other motions, such as turning a page of music, drinking a glass of water or tightening your bow.

Step 8. Move your left arm as if shifting up and down the whole length of your cello's fingerboard.

Step 9. Put your feet together and draw large and small circles.

Do you feel tension when you do not let your body move?

Do you feel stronger when you steer with your feet?

Do you feel stronger with your feet apart or together?

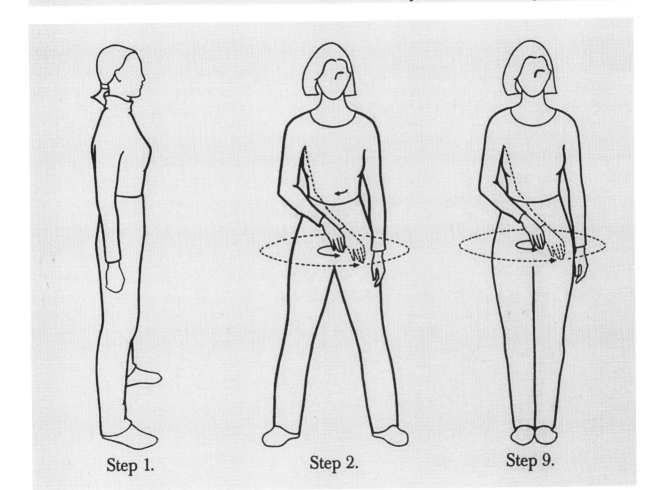

Step 1.   Step 2.   Step 9.

Observations

Even the slightest motion involves your entire body. Although your body may only move a short distance, your arm can move the same or a greater distance in response to the same body impulse. Your arm moves farther to draw a large circle than to draw a small one. Your body, however, moves the same distance, regardless of how large or small a circle you draw.

Because your body is so much heavier than your arm, it is more powerful. Your arm always moves in the opposite direction from your body. When your body moves, your weight shifts from side to side with each motion.

You can immediately feel tension when you move your arm without allowing your body to move. When your body moves freely, however, especially when you steer your body with your feet, you feel strong and free of tension.

You feel strong when you have a broad base. Narrowing your base of support by bringing your feet together weakens you and creates tension.

Chapter Seven
Sources of Physical Power

> "Only this impulse coming from the center of the body instead of each extremity . . . will group different movements in a unified whole."
> —*Pablo Casals*

A common assumption is that muscles are the sole source of the body's power. This assumption puts the cart before the horse, however, because even the strongest person is weak if not well balanced.

Muscles are necessary for the body to function, as are the skeletal, respiratory, circulatory and nervous systems. Each essential body component fulfills its own role in concert with the others.

Balancing Mechanism

Although muscles move the body and its limbs and bones provide a system of levers, the primary source of your body's physical power is the natural shifting of weight, or the *balancing mechanism*. This mechanism coordinates all body parts as they move to perform physical activities.

Your center of gravity is in constant motion, stimulating continual counterbalancing motions. When your body or any of its parts is purposefully moved, counterbalancing motions become more pronounced.

Your center of gravity resides in the heaviest part of your body, your trunk. When balancing a lighter and heavier body part, the heavier part has more power than the lighter part. The dog wags the tail, not the other way around.

When you use this power, your arms react to a body impulse by moving in the opposite direction with great precision. If this process is restricted, however, your muscles are forced to overwork, creating tension. If your balancing mechanism is not restricted, your muscles perform efficiently and work only enough to accomplish the desired motions. This creates no tension.

In a chance encounter I had an interesting conversation with a young boxer. He was obviously excited about what he was learning from his trainer.

"Most people think that the best fighters are the strongest ones," he said. "Not so!" he continued. "It is all a matter of balance and shifting weight. And nothing is more important than your footwork."

I told him that I play and teach the cello, an occupation, seemingly as far removed from his as one could imagine. Yet I teach the very same principles.

Footwork

Most sports stress footwork as an essential part of training. Footwork is equally important for cello playing.

Our feet and legs form the base of support for our bodies. We use our feet to stand on, but this is only one of their functions. Humans cannot fly like birds. We must be connected to the ground to achieve good balance. Lifting away from the pull of gravity requires that we maintain this connection through our feet.

Try sitting upright in a chair with your feet raised slightly off the floor. You will very likely experience considerable stress and find it difficult to remain erect.

Your feet also control the movements of your body as your weight shifts from one side to the other. They form the broadest part of your body's base. Because your feet are farthest away from the rest of your body, they provide the best leverage for steering your body's movements. Remember how your arm movements became stronger when steered by your feet as you drew circles in step 6 of Demonstration 4 on page 38.

It is easier to sense the link between your body and your feet when you stand than when you sit. This is probably why so many cellists (because they sit when they play their instruments) are unaware of the advantages of steering body movements with their feet. Becoming aware can increase physical comfort and improve control.

Demonstration 5

Throwing a Ball

This demonstration explores the natural sequence of body movements which occur when you throw a ball. Consider how this sequence of motion applies to cello playing.

Step 1. Pretend to throw a ball.

Step 2. Notice the sequence and direction of your body movements.

Step 3. Observe what happens to your trunk, legs, feet, upper arms, forearms and hands.

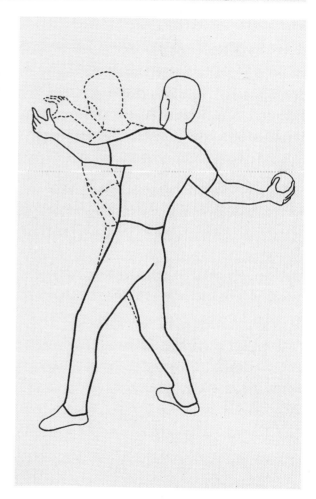

Observations

Each impulse from your body initiates a chain of events. It pulls in the direction of the ball's destination as your arm moves in the opposite direction. Your body moves forward as your arm moves backward. Your body then moves backward as your arm thrusts forward.

Your body weight shifts through each phase of motion. You can feel the power when your body lifts and rotates as you pivot from one foot to the other. This superbly coordinated flow of motion occurs spontaneously in response to your desired action.

As you simulate throwing a ball, the motions of all your limbs depend on impulses from your center of gravity which anticipate your arm movements. Your arm responds by immediately moving in the opposite direction.

When your arm moves, the heaviest part (the upper arm) leads the way, followed by your forearm and your hand in that order. *The sequence of motion is always from the heavier to the lighter part of your body.*

When playing the cello, this natural sequence of motion is sometimes interrupted. Pressing the bow with the fingers or hand, or pressing the fingers of the left hand creates tension that can short circuit this natural flow.

Even the smallest motion involves your entire body. Your body functions as a unified whole rather than a collection of isolated parts. Those who focus too much on small motor movements can easily lose this vital connection with the rest of their body.

Demonstration 6

Press, Push, Lift and Pull

Your body reacts differently to different actions.
Some create tension while others do not.

This demonstration shows how your body
reacts to pressing, pushing, lifting and pulling.
Perform the breath test with each step.

Step 1. Provide resistance with your left hand
as you press lightly against it with a
finger of your right hand. Press somewhat harder.

Step 2. Provide resistance with your left hand
as you push it toward the left with
your right arm.

Step 3. Provide resistance with your left hand
as you pull it toward the right with
your right arm.

Step 4. Provide resistance with your left hand
as you lift it with your right arm.

Do you feel tension in some of the steps?

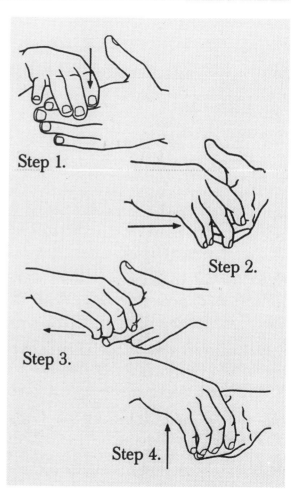

Step 1.

Step 2.

Step 3.

Step 4.

Observations

Even when pressing very lightly you can feel tension radiate up your arm. When you press harder you can feel the tension extend all the way to your back. Pushing is similar to pressing. In effect, it is a similar action moving in a different direction.

Pressing and pushing create tension by causing opposing groups of muscles to contract at the same time. Pressing and pushing also compress the joints.

Lifting and pulling are similarly related. They have the opposite effect from pressing or pushing, however. They allow opposing muscle groups to contract and lengthen normally. Lifting and pulling also keep the joints open, minimize tension and reduce the danger of injury. Pressing and pushing create tension, but pulling and lifting do not.

Many string players believe that they must press to play their instruments. Some even understand that pressing causes tension, but see it as a necessary evil. Evil, yes; necessary, no!

Demonstration 7

Pressing and Lifting at Arm's Length

This demonstration explores the differences between pressing and lifting at arm's length and how they affect your body alignment.

Step 1. Lean forward as you press a string down to play a note near the upper end of the fingerboard.

Step 2. Sit upright and press the string down again in the same place.

Step 3. Sit upright and play the same note by gently pulling or lifting to play on the side of the string.

While sitting upright, is it easier to play at the upper end of the fingerboard by pressing or by playing on the side of the string?

Observations

It is more difficult to press when your left arm is extended than when it is bent. This is why many cellists lean forward, crouch or lean to one side when playing in the upper register. When you eliminate pressing by playing on the side of the string with gentle lifting or pulling movements, it becomes just as easy to play at arm's length as closer to your body.

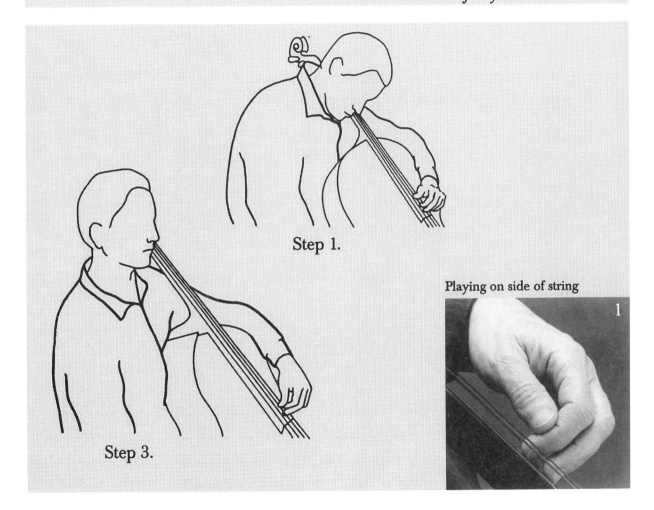

Step 1.

Step 3.

Playing on side of string

1

Demonstration 8

Pressing and Pulling the Bow

This demonstration compares how pressing and pulling affect your bowing. Perform the breath test with each step.

Step 1. Hold your bow as if you are playing at the frog. Rest your bow on your left hand.

Step 2. Press your bow against your left hand as if you are playing at the tip.

Step 3. Pull your bow as you provide resistance with your left hand near the lower part of the bow.

Step 4. Pull your bow as you provide resistance with your left hand at the tip.

Does it require more effort to press your bow down at the tip than at the frog?

Does it require more effort to pull your bow at the tip than at the frog?

Observations

More effort is required to exert pressure at the tip of the bow than at the frog. Pressure must gradually increase as you move toward the upper part of the bow to sustain a tone.

If arm weight rather than pressing is used for tone production, the balance must be constantly readjusted to maintain the right amount of weight at each location on the bow.

Pulling requires the same effort anywhere on the bow. Your arm feels the same regardless of where you encounter resistance. Pulling provides consistent contact or positive traction and eliminates the need to adjust pressure or weight. Pulling is your arm's natural response to your body's weight shifting impulses.

A longtime colleague often quoted his teacher's favorite admonition to his students about pressing: "As more you presses, as less you getses!"

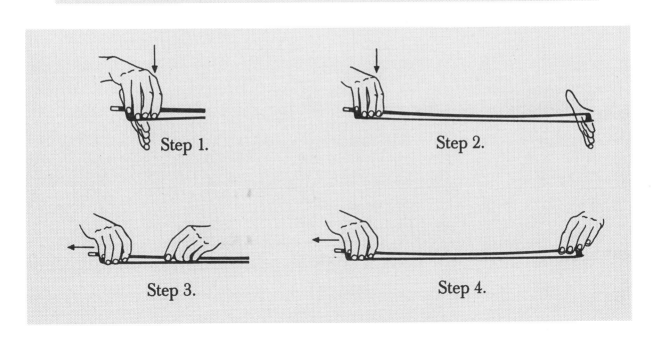

Anything that can be done by pressing and pushing can be done as well or better by pulling and lifting.

Chapter Eight
Sitting

Back pain is a common complaint among the general population. As a group, musicians suffer an even higher rate of back injuries. The rate of back pain among cellists is higher than for any other group of musicians. A major cause of cellists' back pain is faulty sitting.

Sitting is more complicated than standing. Standing permits greater freedom of movement. It allows your body to maintain better balance and to shift your weight naturally as you move your arms.

Standing also provides your body with better leverage because your feet are farther away from your arms than when you are sitting. This is why violinists and other instrumentalists usually prefer to stand when playing solos.

> Archimedes, the ancient Greek mathematician and physicist, explaining to King Hieron how a small force could move a great weight by using a lever, said, "Give me a point of support and I shall move the world."

Learning about the mechanics of sitting is a cellist's first line of defense against back pain.

Sitting and Balance

When sitting, the body's balancing mechanism is less obvious. Contact with the seat obscures the direct connection between the feet and the rest of the body. Unfortunately, many cellists are unaware of how important their feet and legs are for playing their instrument.

Unless the feet can fully support *all* of the body's movements, the body cannot be completely balanced. In addition, when the feet are not properly placed, the knee and hip joints tend to lock, causing a loss of mobility. Later demonstrations will show that better balance and more sensitive control can be achieved by placing the feet farther apart than is customary.

The Anatomy of Sitting

Understanding the anatomy of sitting is a vital first step to re-evaluating your sitting habits. In the past, when cellists suffered back pain from poor seating, little was known about the causes or how to prevent such pain. Today it is not difficult to improve sitting habits and make seats more comfortable.

In his book, *The Musician's Survival Manual*, Dr. Richard N. Norris asks, "When is a chair not a chair?" He answers, "When it is an instrument of torture."[9] He then cites Dr. A.C. Mandel who found that "the human body was not designed to sit with the hips and knees bent at a 90 degree angle."[10] Dr. Norris explains that the thigh bone can only move freely about 60 degrees as it rotates in the hip socket. Moving beyond 60 degrees causes the pelvis to rotate backward.

[9] Norris, R., *The Musician's Survival Manual*. St. Louis: MBB Music, 1993.
[10] Mandel, A.C., *The Seated Man*. Copenhagen: Dafnia Press, 1985.

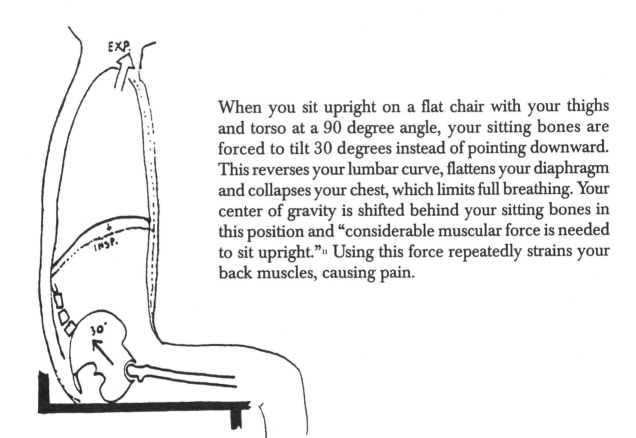

When you sit upright on a flat chair with your thighs and torso at a 90 degree angle, your sitting bones are forced to tilt 30 degrees instead of pointing downward. This reverses your lumbar curve, flattens your diaphragm and collapses your chest, which limits full breathing. Your center of gravity is shifted behind your sitting bones in this position and "considerable muscular force is needed to sit upright."[11] Using this force repeatedly strains your back muscles, causing pain.

Drawing reproduced by permission of Richard Norris, M.D.

[11] Norris, R., *The Musicians's Survival Manual.* St. Louis: MBB Music, 1993.

Demonstration 9

Sitting

This demonstration illustrates how your back is affected by the way your trunk and legs are aligned when you sit. Perform the breath test with each step.

Step 1. Stand tall and hold the back of a chair for support.

Step 2. Lift your knee to bring your thigh to about a 60 degree angle to the floor.

Step 3. Keep your back erect as you slowly raise your knee higher, bringing your thigh parallel to the floor.

Step 4. Release your trunk and let your body slouch forward.

How does your back feel when your thigh is at a 60 degree angle to the floor?

Does your back strain when you hold your thigh parallel to the floor?

Observations

When your thigh is at a 60 degree angle to the floor, you feel no discomfort and can breathe freely. When you hold your thigh parallel to the floor (at a 90 degree angle to your torso), you can immediately feel your pelvis pulling under, straining your lower back. You are unable to breathe freely in this position because your lung capacity is reduced.

Although slouching seems to relieve the strain on your back, it shapes your spine into a letter C, reversing your lumbar curve and weakening your skeletal alignment. When you try to breathe deeply in this position, you find that your lung capacity is diminished.

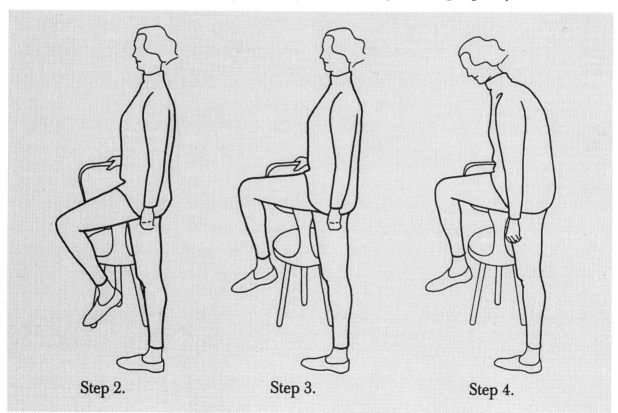

Step 2.   Step 3.   Step 4.

Seat Angle

Have you noticed that most comfortable seats, including car seats, allow your upper body to lean against a back rest? This enlarges the angle between your thighs and trunk and eliminates strain on your lower back.

Because cello playing requires sitting in an upright position, cellists' seats must likewise maintain a wide enough angle between the thighs and trunk to avoid back strain. Your sitting bones can then face comfortably downward and provide the same foundation for your body as when you are standing.

Seat Adjustment

This angle can be achieved by making your seat higher in the back than in the front to allow your knees to be several inches below your hips. It is not necessary to adjust your seat an entire 30 degrees. Most cellists are comfortable with the back of the seat about 15 or 20 degrees higher than the front.

There are several ways to angle your seat. One way is to use a firm, wedge-shaped cushion which is about two-and-one-quarter inches thicker in the back than in the front. Spacers such as books or boards can also be placed under the back legs of your chair to establish the desired angle.

A simple and inexpensive way to improve chairs for music students in schools is to cut lengths of 4 x 4 inch pieces of lumber to fit beneath the back legs of student chairs. Drill two holes in each piece of wood, spacing them far enough apart to receive the chair's legs and deep enough to achieve the desired seat angle. School maintenance departments, wood shop teachers or parent groups are often willing to help out with such a project.

Making this simple seat adjustment is certainly worthwhile because comfortable students play better and enjoy their music making more.

Chair Height

The height of your chair presents another challenge. As Goldilocks discovered, comfortable sitting requires a chair of the proper height. No sitting strategy will help if your chair is too high or too low.

People come in different sizes, but chairs generally do not. Most chairs are manufactured to standard heights and therefore cannot suit everyone.

A chair is the optimal height if it allows you to sit with your knees several inches below your hips. Because standard chairs are too low for many cellists, players with long legs are the most likely to have seating difficulties.

Shorter cellists can often find adequate support by sitting close enough to the front edge of their chairs so that their thighs do not rest on the chair. Shorter student chairs are also available for children and others. Cellists with longer legs need a higher-than-standard seat.

You can raise the height of your chair by using a thicker-than-normal wedge-shaped cushion or by placing a firm flat cushion beneath a standard wedged one.

The Worst Hazard

A seat that slopes backward is the worst hazard of all to a cellist's back. When the back of a seat is lower than the front, gravity constantly pulls the player backward. Muscles are then forced to tense and strain to keep the body upright. Unfortunately, such chairs are frequently found in concert halls, schools and music studios. Cellists can avoid discomfort and the risk of injury by bringing their own tapered cushions or risers when this kind of chair is unavoidable.

State-of-the-art hydraulic chairs with adjustable seats are now available for other professionals who sit at their work. Let us hope that such chairs will soon be designed for musicians.

Orchestra Seating

Orchestras at home and abroad are gradually becoming more aware of the importance of seating. Increasingly, they are providing ergonomically-improved chairs. The Los Angeles Philharmonic, for example, has adapted special chairs for its cello section. These chairs have forward-sloping seats and are set at different heights to accommodate the needs of each individual player.

In 1994 the California Chapter of the American String Teachers Association launched an educational campaign to provide information about musicians' seating problems to the musical community. This campaign targets professional musicians, students, amateur musicians and music educators.

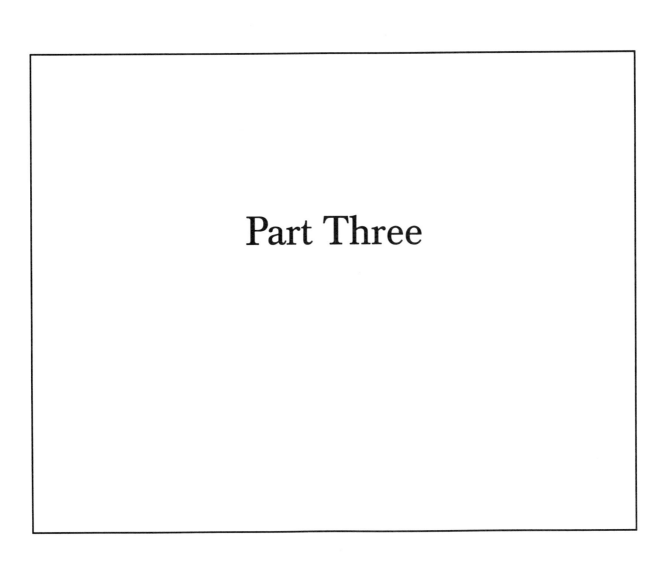

Part Three

Chapter Nine
Aligning Your Body and Cello

> "Even the simplest movements of the arms can be carried out properly only when the position of the legs is correspondingly correct."
> — *Carl Flesch*

Cellists are taught to sit in many different ways. Some tuck their feet behind their knees, causing their trunks to lean forward. Teachers of this method usually tell students to sit so that they can stand up instantly. Some are taught to hold the cello so firmly between their legs that it cannot be dislodged by someone trying to take it away.

Others learn to sit upright with their legs straight down from the knees. Some place one foot forward and one foot back or use combinations of various positions. Both tradition and common practice lead most cellists to hold the cello between their legs or knees and to maintain physical contact with both sides of the instrument.

Demonstration 10

Foot Placement When Sitting

This demonstration explores different foot placements without the cello. Perform the breath test with each step.

Step 1. Sit tall on the front edge of your chair and place your feet:

- behind your knees;
- straight down from your knees; and
- various distances in front of your knees.

Step 2. Test each position by moving your trunk forward and backward. Find the position which feels most comfortable and stable.

Step 3. Sit tall with your feet in front of your knees. Experiment with the distance between your feet. Place your feet as if each leg is touching the side of your cello. Move your feet apart a little at a time.

Step 4. Test each position by circling your trunk in all directions. Readjust the distance between your feet to find the most comfortable and stable position.

Step 5. Repeat Step Three as you move your right arm to simulate full bow strokes.

How does the most comfortable position in this demonstration compare to the way you usually sit with your cello?

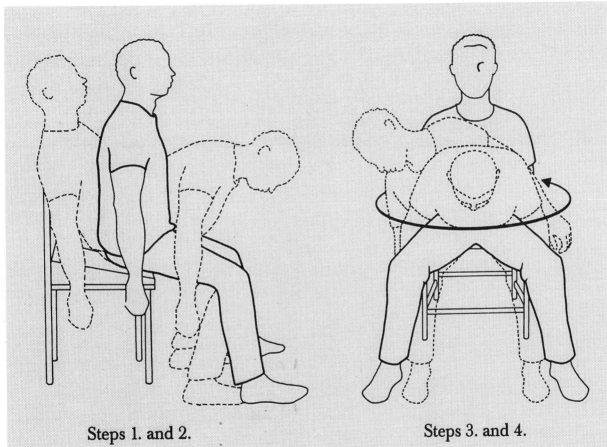

Steps 1. and 2.   **Steps 3. and 4.**

Observations

When you sit with your feet behind your knees, you tend to lean forward. This widely practiced position places extra weight in front of your center of gravity, forcing your back and abdominal muscles to strain to prevent your trunk from falling forward.

In addition, this position misaligns your shoulder joints and encourages you to lift or pull your shoulders forward, especially when playing in the upper registers. Your shoulders are optimally aligned when your body is erect rather than leaning forward. Placing your feet behind your knees also restricts the free movement of your knee and hip joints.

When your feet are straight down from your knees your lower back still strains, although somewhat less than when your feet are behind your knees. Better stability and comfort are maintained when your feet are somewhat in front of your knees. Your balance is strongest with this foot placement. As you test each position in steps three and four, you find the greatest stability and comfort when your feet are considerably farther apart than the width of your cello.

Most cellists would agree that balance is important and that the entire body is involved in playing. Yet most of us play from a base that is too narrow to support our bowing movements or to allow for optimal body balance.

Widening the distance between your feet can make playing substantially easier. This alignment provides a broad enough base to maintain the best balance. It also allows your legs to support the entire span of your bow strokes.

Can you think of any other activity in which you would continually reach your arm away from your body and not try to support it by readjusting your legs? Yet this is an almost universal practice among cellists.

> "It is universally recognized that a capacity for easy transference of weight from foot to foot is the correct foundation for arm movement."[12]
>
> —*Percival Hodgson*

Holding the Cello

The way you sit and hold the cello affects your physical comfort and playing style. Faulty alignment can be artistically limiting and also lead to pain. The effects of poor alignment often worsen over time due to cumulative wear and tear on your body.

Although cellists hold their instruments differently, most center their cellos between their legs. This places the bridge–the cello's bowing area–in line with or close to the center of their body. Some cellists use a higher or lower endpin than others. Cellists position their fingerboard closer, farther or at different angles to their neck. But the most universal practice is to align the cello with the center of the body.

Is this the best arrangement or are there better alternatives?

[12] Hodgson,P., *Motion Study and Violin Bowing*. American String Teachers Association, Urbana: 1958, (First Published, London, 1934)

Demonstration 11

Testing Leverage and Alignment With a Chair

This demonstration illustrates how placing your cello affects the leverage of your bow arm. Using a chair allows you to feel the difference between alignments before testing them with your cello.

Step 1. Stand, facing the side of a chair. Let the chair seat face your left as you stand with the back of the chair in line with the center of your body.

Step 2. Rock the chair gently about 40 or 45 degrees to the right with your right arm.

Step 3. Move to the right so that the center of your body is about six to eight inches to the right of the chair back.

Step 4. Rock the chair back and forth as in step two.

Where is it easier to move the chair?

Where do you find better leverage?

Observations

Rocking the chair is easier when the center of your body is to the right of the chair. It is harder to rock the chair when it is in line with the center of your body. Reaching to the left with your right arm provides better leverage than reaching to the center of your body.

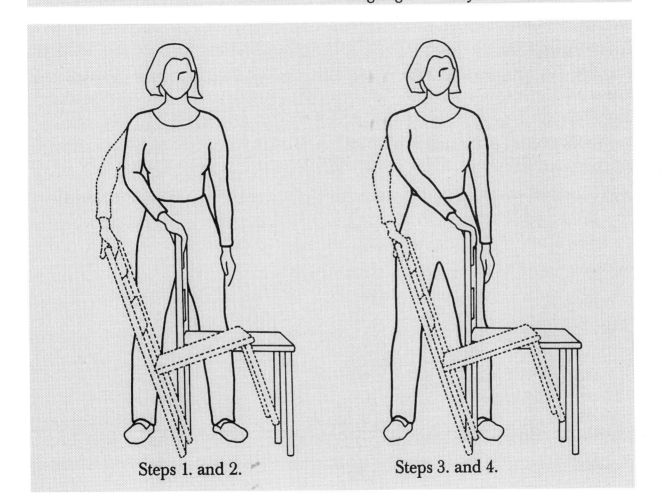

Steps 1. and 2.   Steps 3. and 4.

Demonstration 12

Alignment With the Cello

This demonstration explores how the location of your cello affects the leverage of your bow arm.

Step 1. Hold your cello on the left side of your body. Take several bow strokes beginning at the frog.

Step 2. Move your cello so that the bridge is in line with the center of your body. Take several bow strokes as you did in step one.

Where do you find the best leverage?

Where does your bow arm feel most comfortable?

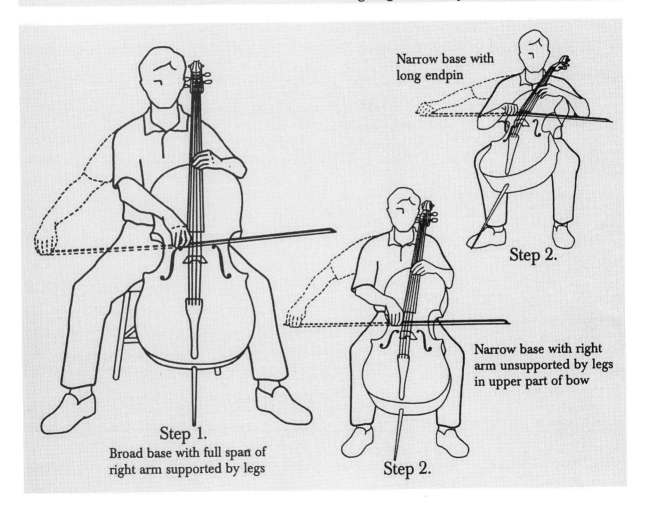

Narrow base with
long endpin

Step 2.

Step 1.
Broad base with full span of
right arm supported by legs

Narrow base with right
arm unsupported by legs
in upper part of bow

Step 2.

Observations

Keeping the bridge or bowing area well to the left of the center of your body has a number of significant advantages. Just as it is easier to rock a chair when it is on your left, it is easier to bow with your cello on the left side of your body. This placement provides better leverage. Your entire body is more open, which allows your body's balance mechanism to function more freely.

In this position, your bow arm is less cramped and you do not have to reach as far to the right to use the upper part of your bow. This alone can dramatically reduce the risk of right arm tendinitis which is so common among cellists.

This position is also more effective because the entire span of your bow stroke is supported by your feet and legs. It eliminates the common tendency of some, to move their right elbow behind their back to play on the C string. With your cello to the left of the center of your body, you do not have to raise your bow arm as high to play on the A string. In addition, this position gives your left arm better access to your instrument.

Have you ever noticed where violinists or violists hold their instruments? They hold them on the left side of their bodies. Some players hold their instruments farther to the left than others, but none keep the bridge in line with the center of their bodies. Imagine the twisted positions that would result if they did.

When cellists keep their bridges in line with, or even close to, the center of their bodies, similar twisting occurs. This twisting can be more difficult to discern because of the cello's larger size. Nevertheless, twisting takes its toll. It is the body that needs to be centered, not the cello.

The History of Cello Placement

The practice of centering the cello evolved before the endpin was invented. In those days cellists usually cradled their instrument between the calves of their legs, emulating viola da gamba players. This brought the bridge of their instrument toward the center of their body. The illustration of Luigi Boccherini on page 74 is probably quite typical of how most cellists held their instruments in that era.

Boccherini, however, did not have the problem of insufficient support for his right arm when he played at the upper part of his bow. This is because he effectively shortened his bow by holding it a considerable distance above the frog.

Although Jean Louis Duport and Boccherini were contemporaries, Duport was a notable exception to the prevailing practice of centering his cello. He held his instrument well to the left side of his body. Notice how comfortable and stable he appears in the illustration on page 75.

Duport used a longer and more advanced bow than Boccherini, but one that still pre-dated the modern bow. Yet, because of the way he aligned his cello and held his bow (above the frog), he had better support for his bow arm than many present-day cellists.

In his comprehensive book about cello playing, Duport instructs the readers, "Put your left foot far from yourself and in front . . . the weight of the cello is carried at the side of the left leg. The left foot is outside. The right leg is placed on the bottom of the side-piece of the cello to hold the instrument securely."[13]

Compare Duport's alignment to the way most cellists hold their instrument today.

[13] Duport, J.L. *Essai sur le Doigte du Violoncelle et la conduite de l'archet, avec une suite d'exercices*, Paris 1819. Translated by Nancy Stein.

Luiggi Boccherini
1743-1805

Reproduced by permission of the National Gallerey of Victoria, Australia

Jean Louis Duport
1749-1819

Development of the Modern Bow

The problems caused by extending the right arm away from the body without support from the legs and feet began with the development of the modern bow and the practice of holding it at the frog.

With changing times, string players sought stronger sounding instruments. As concert halls became larger, the demand for greater sound projection continued. The bows used by Boccherini and Duport no longer sufficed. The stronger modern bow, standardized by Francois Tourte (1747-1835), allowed string players to sustain longer tones and to play with greater power.

This transition also brought changes to the cello. The instrument's neck was made longer. Bridges were raised to provide greater string pressure on the top of the cello. Stronger sound posts and bass bars were added to support this increased pressure.

Although bows and instruments were strengthened to meet changing musical requirements, the way most cellists align their instrument has not yet fully adapted to this improved equipment.

Broadening the base and moving the cello to the left side of the body can offer relief from much of the physical stress commonly experienced by cellists. Shortly after the advantage of this alignment became apparent to me, I was delighted to discover the picture of Jean Louis Duport in a book called *The Cello Story* by Dimitry Markevitch. Duport played with his cello on the left side of his body almost two hundred years ago. Yet few have followed his example.

Necessity, the Mother of Invention

Adrien Francois Servais (1807-1885) is credited with inventing the cello endpin. Although many cellists played without an endpin well into the early part of the 20th century, its use is virtually universal today.

Servais played without an endpin throughout most of his career, as was the custom of his time. According to an account in the Grove's Dictionary of Music and Musicians, Servais became so stout toward the end of his life that he had difficulty holding his cello. Using an endpin provided him with needed relief.

Placing and Holding the Cello

Optimal cello placement provides comfortable and stable support for all body movements. It is well-balanced and allows free access to all regions of the instrument.

Demonstration 13

Placing the Cello

This demonstration explores ways to find your own optimal cello placement.

Step 1. Place your cello on the left side of your body, resting on three points: the floor (through the end-pin), the left side of your chest and your left knee.

Step 2. Experiment with the amount of space between your right leg and your cello. Make the span wide enough to completely support your body and your bow-arm when you play at the tip of the bow.

Step 3. Experiment with the angle of your cello to find the greatest comfort. Find a position that is flexible and allows you to rotate your cello easily with a slight motion of your left knee.

Step 4. Expand your lungs with your body erect, so that you can breathe deeply. Be sure to always keep your shoulders behind your cello.

Step 5. Balance on the heel and ball of each foot.

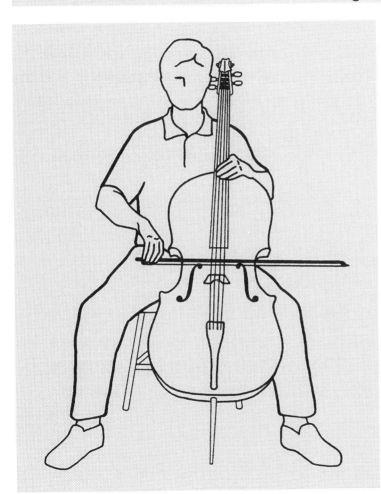

Observations

Placing your cello on the left side of your body with your right leg well away from the side of your instrument provides the best alignment. Your body is balanced and flexible and all of your playing motions are fully supported. You can access all regions of your cello without slouching, twisting or leaning forward. You may feel as if you are *semi-standing* when you sit this way.

Demonstration 14

Aligning the Cello With the Left Side of Your Body

This demonstration guides you in aligning your cello to the left side of your body. First perform steps one through four without your cello. After you find the most comfortable alignment, pick up your cello and proceed to step five. Perform the breath test with each step.

Step 1. Hold your left hand at various distances from your neck to find the most comfortable alignment.

Step 2. Hold your left hand at various distances from your shoulder to find the most comfortable alignment.

Step 3. Move your left arm forward and down in line with your shoulder as if traversing the length of your fingerboard.

Step 4. Move your left arm toward your right as if traversing the entire length of your fingerboard.

Step 5. When you find the most comfortable path for your left arm, set your cello so that your fingerboard is in line with this path.

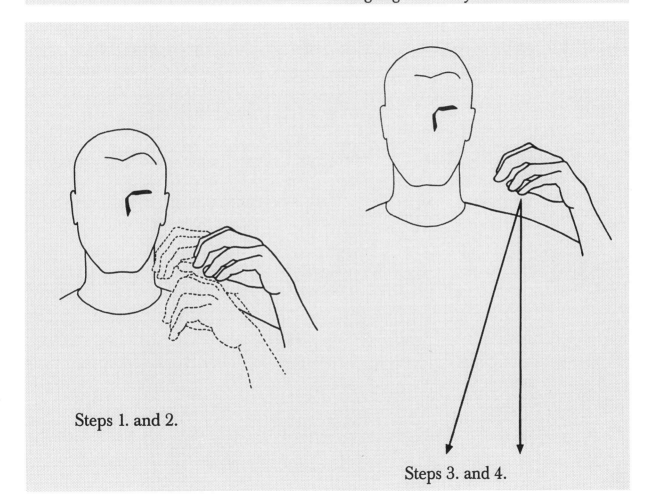

Steps 1. and 2.

Steps 3. and 4.

Observations

You will probably find that you are most comfortable when your arm is rather open, with plenty of space between your hand, neck and shoulder. When your arm is open and in line with your shoulder you are able to extend your arm completely and easily. You do not feel an impulse to lean forward, to pull your shoulder forward or up or to twist your body.

This position gives you access to the entire range of your fingerboard without distorting your body's alignment. If your arm is too close to your neck or shoulder it tends to be cramped, especially when you play in the lower registers. It also encourages you to lean forward or raise your shoulder when you play in the upper registers.

By using this alignment your body can remain comfortably erect and you can play easily in all registers. You will have no inclination to lean forward or to one side, or to bend or lift your shoulders—practices which put you at constant risk of pain or injury.

You will also find that the best alignment of your fingerboard and left arm closely corresponds to the optimal position you found when aligning your body and your cello for bowing. Minor adjustments may be needed, however, to accommodate your particular size and body build.

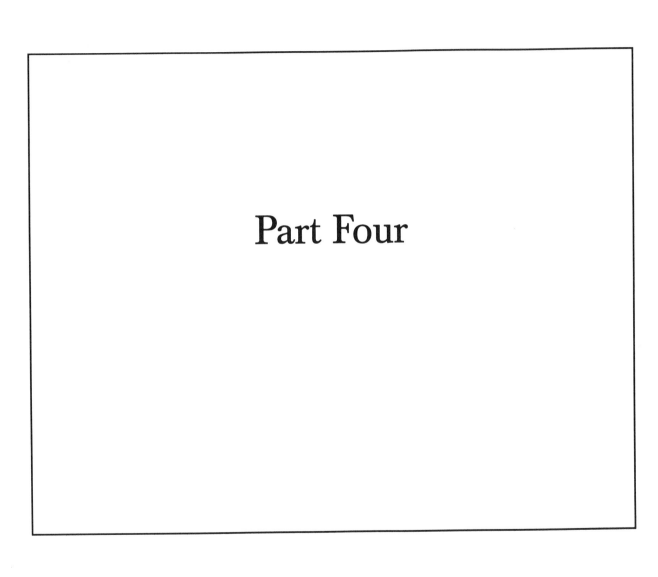

Part Four

Chapter Ten
Bowing

The Inevitability of Curves

In 1934, Percival Hodgson published photographic recordings showing the path of the right hand in bowings. He created cyclegraphs which trace the patterns of motion in a wide variety of bowing patterns. These cyclegraphs show curves, circles, ovals, figure eights, loops and every manner of squiggle. They illustrate everything but straight lines or square corners. They provide "... convincing proof of the inevitability of curves."[14]

Cyclegraphs of different individuals performing the same actions might vary from person to person. Yet the basic shapes and patterns are similar. This is like penmanship. Although individual handwritings may differ, one can still read what another has written.

[14] Hodgson, P., *Motion Study and Violin Bowing*. American String Urbana: American String Teachers Association, 1958.

The inevitability of curves applies not only to bowing, but to all body movements. Although cyclegraphs show curves in only one dimension, human bodies move along more complex paths. Bodies and limbs naturally curve in several directions at one time, largely in spirals. This can be easily observed in either commonplace or highly-refined activities. For example, if you stop reading this page for a moment and reach for an imaginary object you will find that your arm moves in a curved or spiral path.

I find it valuable to show Hodgson's pictures to every student who enters my studio. They help string players at all levels to see these visual images of bowing motions. They are accurate representations of the reality of body movement and reveal the natural choreography of bowing.

See pages 88 and 89 for examples of Hodgson's cyclegraphs and the types of bowing movements they represent. The cyclegraphs are reproduced as originally published with musical examples written for the violin. The principles they demonstrate, however, are equally applicable to all bowed instruments.

"There are no straight bows."
—*Leonard Rose*

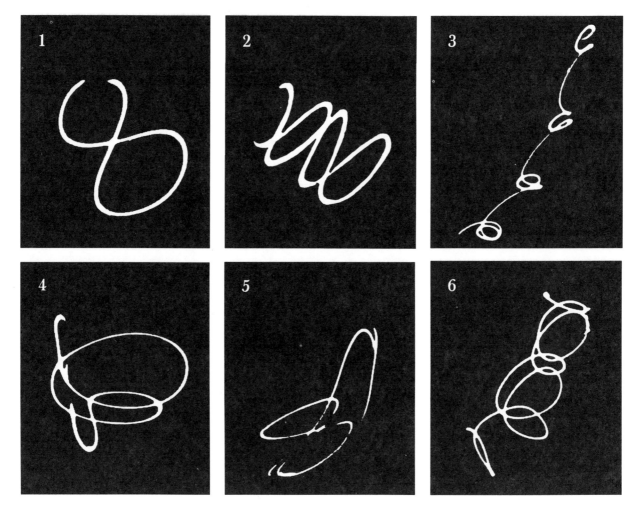

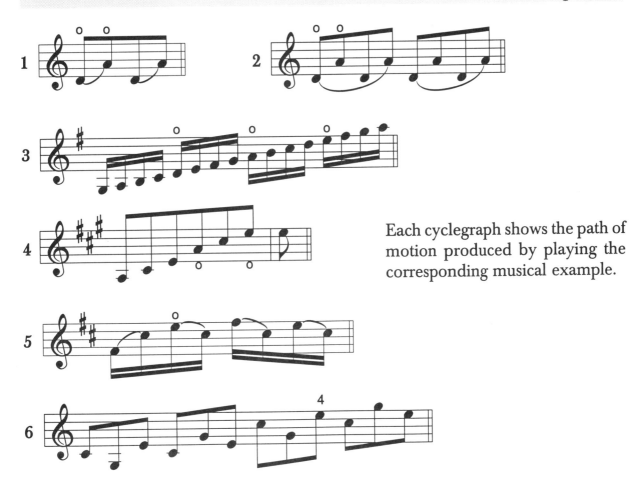

Each cyclegraph shows the path of motion produced by playing the corresponding musical example.

Cyclegraphs and musical examples are reproduced by permission of the American String Teachers Association.

Demonstration 15
Straight and Curved Bowing

This demonstration illustrates the differences between straight and curved bowing. Perform the breath test with each step.

Step 1. Simulate vigorous bowing in straight lines.

Step 2. Simulate bowing in circles, ovals, spirals, figure eights and other curved paths.

How does your body respond to moving in straight lines?

How does it feel to move in curved paths?

Which is easier and more comfortable?

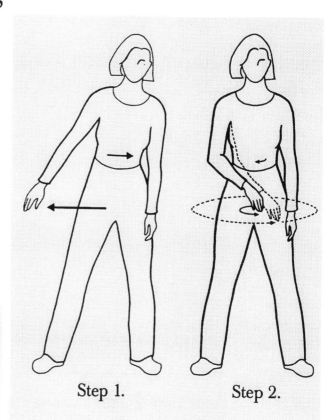

Step 1.   Step 2.

Observations

You feel a jolt at the end of each stroke when you move in straight lines. This occurs when motion in one direction is interrupted to reverse direction. Abrupt stopping forces opposing muscles to contract at the same time, causing tension. Putting on the brakes is more difficult than continuing motion. Abrupt movements can also stress your joints and back.

When your arms move in straight lines your body also moves in straight lines. This causes your body to move a greater distance than for curved motions. The breath test reveals that breathing is restricted with straight movements but not with curved ones.

Natural motions are always curved and continuous. They include preparation and follow-through. Preparatory motions preceding bow strokes, shifts or any other movements break the inertia of being at a standstill. Follow-through completes each motion to avert sudden stops.

Demonstration 16

Path of Bow

Once you recognize the curved nature of bowing motions you will also observe that curves move in one direction or the other, either clockwise or counterclockwise.

This demonstration illustrates the direction of down-bows and up-bows.

Step 1. Swing your right arm to draw several loose counterclockwise circles. Perform these motions with abandon, allowing your arm to find its path of least resistance.

Step 2. Swing your right arm to draw several loose clockwise circles. Again allow your arm to find its path of least resistance.

Observations

The half of each circle closest to your body is the part of each bow stroke that touches the string. Down-bows move counterclockwise and up-bows move clockwise.

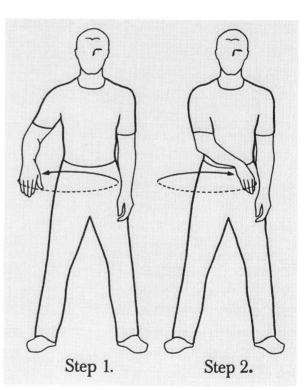

Step 1.   Step 2.

Angle of Bow Contact

The angle of the bow's contact with the strings affects the ease of tone production. Leaning forward to press or to direct arm and body weight downward engages the bow at an oblique angle to the string. This requires the use of greater force than when the bow moves more directly toward the string. Gravity and the natural arc of the arm can bring the bow toward the string at a more favorable angle when sitting upright .

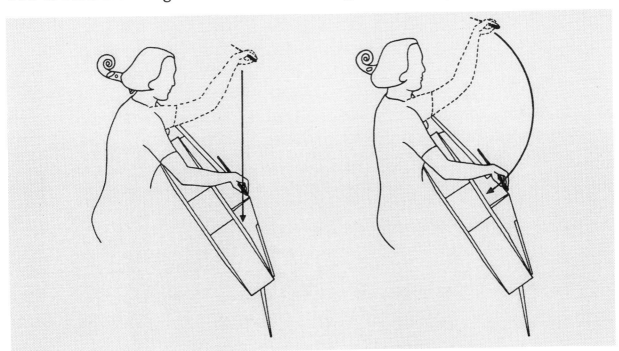

Demonstration 17
Angle of Bow

It is widely assumed that the bow must always be straight and parallel to the bridge. It is neither completely possible nor necessarily desirable, however, to always keep the bow straight. This demonstration explores the differences between straight and angled bowing.

Step 1. Play a short down-bow with the tip of your bow pointing slightly upward toward the fingerboard. Pull your bow across the string at about a 90 degree angle to the string. (In line with the arrow.)

Step 2. Play an up-bow with the tip of your bow pointing slightly downward toward the floor. Move your bow at about a 90 degree angle to the string. (In line with the arrow.)

Step 3. Play a down-bow and an up-bow, keeping your bow at a 90 degree angle to the string.

Can you draw a more focused sound when the bow is straight or angled?

Which feels better?

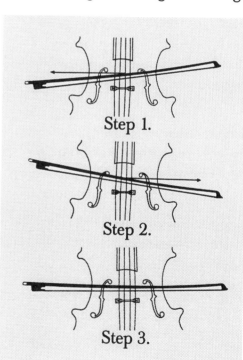

Step 1.

Step 2.

Step 3.

Observations

Pointing the tip of the bow slightly upward on down-bows and downward on up-bows creates greater friction than when the bow is at a right angle to the string. This friction provides a solid point of contact as your arm responds to your body's weight-shifts in the opposite direction. Your arm's natural response to these weight shifts is to pull the bow. This greater friction provides a resistance, or something to pull. Playing this way completely eliminates pressing or pushing the bow.

Allowing your bow's angle to vary requires less effort than trying to it keep it straight and parallel to the bridge. Because these movements are naturally curved, they are more comfortable and tension-free.

This approach draws a quicker response from the instrument and produces a more focused and controllable sound. This is particularly noticeable when playing near the upper end of the fingerboard where the vibrating string length is short.

The angle at which the bow crosses the string does not have to be exactly as shown in the illustrations. It may vary considerably depending on your personal preferences and requirements of the music. It is especially helpful, however, to angle your bow at the beginning of a stroke.

Demonstration 18

Bowing Arm Level

Maintaining the proper arm level for each bow stroke enables you to consistently produce your best sound. It also allows you to make seamless bow changes with the least effort and alleviates tension. As you will see in this demonstration, the optimal arm level at any moment depends on which string is being used, the direction of the bow stroke and the direction of string crossings.

Step 1. Play measure one. Keep your arm at the same level for all of the notes. Round the ends of your strokes to form figure eights as you connect one stroke with the next.

Step 2. Play measure two using your whole arm to change strings.

Step 3. Play measure three, keeping your arm at the same level until the slurred up-bow. Pivot your whole arm up to the D string as you play the fifth note. Drop your arm to the level you used on the first three notes before you play the sixth note.

Step 4. Play measure four with your arm at the lower level for down-bows and at the upper level for up-bows. Allow your bow to circle around the string so that you play down-bows on the left side of the string and up-bows on the right side.

Observations

Two arm levels are used on each string. One level is used for up-bows and another level is used for down-bows. When you play consecutive strokes on a single string, therefore, your arm level changes for each stroke. It is lower for down-bows and higher for up-bows. Rounding the ends of your strokes to form figure eights connects the counterclockwise down-bows with the clockwise up-bows.

Your arm remains at the same level for all strokes when you alternate between two neighboring strings with down-bows on the upper string and up-bows on the lower. This is because the down-bow level on the upper string is the same as the up-bow level on the adjacent lower string.

Your arm level must change when you use an up-bow on the upper string and a down-bow on the lower to alternate between strings. Your arm must travel far enough to be at the up-bow level of the upper string and at the down-bow level of the lower string.

If your arm is at the same level for both down-bows and up-bows on the same string, one of the strokes tends to be weaker than the other. When you change levels appropriately you can confidently produce an equally good sound in both directions. This is also the easiest way to perform seamless bow changes.

Up-bow and Down-bow

In this book *down-bow position* refers to angling your bow so that the tip points upward. *Up-bow position* refers to angling your bow so that the tip points downward.

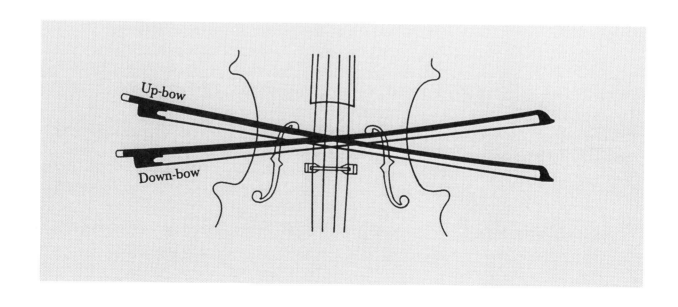

Preparatory Motions

Every act you perform includes preparation. When you throw a ball, your arm moves *backward* to prepare to throw the ball *forward.*

A preparatory motion usually moves in the opposite direction from the intended one. Preparatory motions are essential to all movement because they break the inertia of being at a standstill. In other words, you must be in motion before the beginning of any purposeful motion.

This is a natural, involuntary impulse and occurs with all movements, including bowing, shifting, fingering, extensions, contractions and vibrato. Immobility upsets body balance and causes tension. Allowing for natural preparatory motions, therefore, eliminates tension and makes playing easier.

Demonstration 19

Preparatory Motions in Bowing

This demonstration explores preparatory motions in bowing.

Step 1. Prepare to play a down-bow by placing your arm at an up-bow level (as if you have just completed an up-bow stroke). Release your arm quickly, allowing it to drop to the down-bow level before you play your down-bow.

Step 2. Play a down-bow, keeping your arm at the down-bow level throughout the stroke.

Step 3. Prepare to play an up-bow by placing your arm at the down-bow level (as if you have just completed a down-bow stroke). Circle your arm gradually and lift it to the up-bow level before you play the up-bow stroke.

Step 4. Play an up-bow with your arm at the up-bow level throughout the stroke.

Step 5. Play alternating down-bow and up-bow strokes. Prepare each stroke by being at the arm level for each new stroke before you change direction. Strive to make your motions and sound continuous.

Step 6. Play several strokes in each direction without preparatory motions.

How does playing with preparatory motions sound?

How does playing with preparatory motions feel?

Observations

Bowing with preparatory motions sounds and feels better because it is more in tune with your body's natural impulses. It creates the optimal alignment for each phase of your bowing motions. When you continue to alternate up and down-bows, each stroke naturally prepares for the succeeding one.

Be sure to maintain appropriate arm levels throughout each stroke until it is time to prepare to reverse direction. Using the correct arm level at the right time enables you always to produce your best sound with the least effort.

Demonstration 20

Shape of Rapid Bow Strokes

Repeated rapid bow strokes require different choreography than longer strokes. Because rapid notes do not allow enough time for figure eights, they are shaped like a series of small spiraling ovals. Play these rapid bow strokes:

Step 1. Play measure one at a rapid tempo.

Step 2. Play measure two at a rapid tempo.

Do you feel the clockwise circular movement in measure one?

Do you feel the counterclockwise circular movement in measure two?

Does it take more effort to move clockwise or counterclockwise?

Does your arm need to move a greater distance when bowing in one direction than the other?

Observations

When alternating rapidly between two strings, it is easier to play down-bows on the upper string and up-bows on the lower string for two reasons. In this sequence your arm remains on the same level for both strings. In addition, your arm moves in a clockwise direction and clockwise circles are more natural when you use your right arm.

Think of your first impulse when you stir a cup of coffee or bowl of cereal with your right hand. You are most likely to stir in a clockwise direction. When you stir with your left hand, you tend to use a counterclockwise motion.

This is not to say that you cannot make counterclockwise circles with your right arm. It is essential to be able to circle the bow in both directions. It is important to understand, however, that counterclockwise movements with your right arm require a bit more effort. When you appreciate the difference between moving in one direction and the other you are equipped to cope with all varieties of bowing.

Using clockwise motions whenever possible makes it easier to perform the so-called *Vivaldi bowings*, which alternate rapidly between two strings.

Vivaldi, Concerto in D, Third movement, Allegro vivace

Demonstration 21

Body Impulses and Rapid Bowing

For separate rapid notes, either on or off the string, several notes are played in response to a single body impulse. The first note of each group begins this pattern and successive notes rebound from the same impulse.

Step 1. Play measure one with short down-bows near the middle of your bow. Initiate each stroke with a body impulse, rotating your body in the opposite direction. Steer your body with your right foot.

Step 2. Using the same body impulse, play the two short notes in measure two. Allow your bow to rebound to play the second note.

Step 3. Play three, then four note groups. Allow notes after the first in a group to rebound.

Step 4. Play a short up-bow near the middle of the bow. Initiate the stroke with your body rotating in the opposite direction. Steer your body with your left foot. Continue to experiment with two, three and four note groups.

Step 5. Rotate your body back and forth to play continuing four note groups beginning with a down-bow. Re-energize your body movement with your right foot on the first note of every other group.

Step 6. Rotate your body as in step five. Play continuing up-bow groups, re-energizing the beginning of every other group with your left foot.

Step 7. Play the groups of triplets in measure five. Rotate your body in the opposite direction to the first note of each group.

Observations

Two, three, four, six or eight note groups can be played from the same starting impulse. Additional strokes continue to rebound after an initial body impulse in the opposite direction on the first note of each group. Subsequent notes are re-energized by body impulses with the first note of each group.

For example, when a passage of rapid sixteenth notes begins with a down-bow, your body impulse rotates in the opposite direction—to the left—with the first note of each group. If the group of notes begins with an up-bow, your body impulse is to the right.

Although body impulses are very small when playing rapid short notes, they are essential to avoid the tension produced by complete immobility.

Steering with your feet is a good way to get started and to become aware of the direction of the impulses. With practice, active steering becomes unnecessary. It is replaced by a sense of natural balance and buoyancy.

Demonstration 22

Bow Angles in Rapid Bowing

This demonstration explores the bow angles needed for rapid bow strokes.

Step 1. Play rapid repeated notes on the string in the middle of the bow:

- with your bow at a right angle to the string;

- in a down-bow position; and

- in an up-bow position.

Step 2. Play rapid repeated notes off the string:

- with your bow at a right angle to the string;

- in an up-bow position; and

- in a down-bow position.

Which angle works best on the string?

Which angle works best off the string?

Observations

It is easier to play tremolos and smooth, rapid, on-the-string notes in an up-bow position—the tip pointing downward—for all strokes regardless of their direction. In this setting, the bow tends to cling to the string.

All spiccato, sautille or other strokes that *sound* off the string, work best using a down-bow position—with the tip pointing upward. In this setting the bow tends to jump or flutter on the string. The down-bow position works equally well for slow and rapid off-the-string strokes.

Slow Bows

Slow bows are difficult to perform if your body is immobile while your arm is in motion. This upsets your essential body balance. You can avoid immobility when playing a slow bow by rotating your body back and forth as if you are playing a succession of short strokes. The motion of your arm is renewed by each body impulse. In a sense, a slow bow stroke is built upon a sequence of shorter strokes.

This is similar to rolling a tire down the street. Once it is in motion only a gentle, periodic nudge is needed to keep the tire moving at the same speed. In the same way, each body impulse moving opposite to your bow refreshes and re-energizes your bow arm.

These body movements may be only slight impulses, but they enable you to produce a robust sound in any part of the bow *without pressing*. This approach makes your arm feel as if it is floating and makes drawing a slow bow stroke seem effortless.

Demonstration 23

Slow Bows

This demonstration illustrates how to eliminate tension in slow bowing.

Step 1. Stand and draw a series of counterclockwise loops in the air, spiraling your right arm to the right. Initiate this motion by rotating your body in the opposite direction from your arm.

Step 2. Continue the same body rotations as in step one as you move your right arm slowly to the right in one steady motion, as if playing a long, slow stroke.

Step 3. Move your right arm slowly to the right again, without allowing your body to move.

Step 4. Repeat steps one and two, reversing the direction of your arm and body movements.

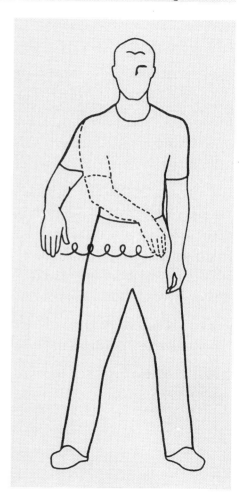

Step 5. Play measure one making continuous counterclockwise loops with your bow. Steer your body movements with your feet. Allow your bow arm to react to your body's movements.

Step 6. Play measure two with a down-bow. Continue the same body movements you used in step five.

Step 7. Play measure two without continuing your body movements.

Step 8. Repeat steps five and six with up-bows, reversing the direction of your bow and body movements.

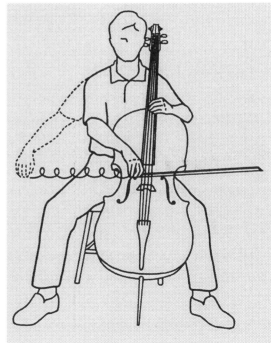

Does your slow bow stroke feel better with or without continuing body movements?

Does your slow bow stroke sound better with or without continuing body movements?

Observations

When you move your arm very slowly without continuous weight shifting, your body reaches a point of immobility while your arm is still moving.

Allowing your body to remain immobile, even for a short period of time, short-circuits your essential balancing mechanism and creates tension. This is why slow playing can seem so difficult.

Some students are taught to play long whole notes as their first bowing experience. This requires beginning students to master a more difficult skill first, which can set the stage for tense playing.

Teachers can instead, introduce students to the joys of cello playing in a tension-free manner by teaching body movements first. They can then introduce short bow strokes connected to these body movements. Once this connection is established, students will be able to master longer strokes easily without pressing, tension or pain.

Consonants and Vowels

Musical sounds are connected or separated in many ways. In music, as in speech, articulation includes vowels and consonants. Smooth legato sounds correspond to vowels, while staccato or accented sounds are musical consonants. Although cellists often press their bows to play staccato and accented notes, these strokes can be performed equally well, or better, without pressing.

Demonstration 24

Single Staccato and Accented Notes

This demonstration illustrates a tension-free way to play single staccato or accented notes.

Step 1. Play a single down-bow staccato note in a down-bow position. Rotate your body to the left, steering with your right foot. Allow your bow arm to react to your body movement. Guide your bow in a counterclockwise direction and play on the left side of the string.

Step 2. Continue to play single staccato notes. Allow your bow arm to make short, spiraling, counterclockwise loops, advancing toward the tip of the bow in small steps. Steer your body to the left with your right foot as you play each note. Rotate your body to the right to prepare for each new note.

Step 3. Play up-bow staccato notes with your bow in an up-bow position. Make spiraling clockwise loops as you steer your body with your left foot.

How does this approach compare with your usual way of playing staccato or accented notes?

Observations

Many string players assume that staccato notes require pressing the bow into the string. This demonstration shows that when staccato strokes are connected to body movements, they require no pressing at all.

A staccato stroke is just a small piece of a legato stroke. You can play more sharply accented notes by using shorter or more abrupt body impulses. Your bow arm responds to your body's impulses to produce a sound and then to release it.

Consciously steering with your feet helps you make the connection between your body and bow strokes. Once established, this process will occur without conscious thought. Your body impulses do not have to be very large. They may be visible or may only be felt as an almost imperceptible feeling of vibrancy.

Continuous Staccato

Continuous and single staccato notes use the same initial impulses. The only difference is that more than one note is played for each body movement in continuous staccato. Each note following the first in a group is driven by rebounding from the initial impulse. As the speed of the staccato is increased the amount of bow used for each note becomes shorter. This allows more notes to rebound in response to each body impulse.

Flexibility can be maintained by moving the bow slightly around the string so that each consecutive note is played in a slightly different place on the circumference of the string. This is easily done by guiding the bow in a spiral path with gentle, undulating movements.

For example, when playing four note groups of up-bow staccato, visualize playing the first note on the right side of the string. Play the second note a bit to the left of the first, and the third note to the left of the second. Play the fourth note approximately where the second note was played. The same sequence begins anew with the first note of the next group.

Down-Bow   Up-Bow

Demonstration 25

Continuous Staccato

This demonstration illustrates how body movements are used to play continuous staccato.

Step 1. Play two consecutive up-bow staccato notes with the same body impulse. Steer your body to the right with your left foot. Allow your bow to rebound to play the second note. Guide the second note around the circumference of the string, playing a little to the left of where you played the first note.

Step 2. Play two consecutive down-bow staccato notes on the same body impulse. Steer your body to your left with your right foot. Allow your arm to rebound to play the second note. Guide your bow around the circumference of the string playing the second note a little to the right of where you played the first note.

Step 3. Experiment with three and four note staccato groups in each direction. Allow succeeding notes to rebound from the first note of each group. Guide the bow around the string so that each successive note in a group is played at a slightly different place on the circumference of the string.

Observations

As your arm rebounds to play repeated staccato notes, it partially released between notes. This releasing action separates a continuous sound into segments. This generates far less tension than pressing downward, pinching the bow or stiffening the arm to produce staccato with involuntary spasms.

Continuous staccato can also be performed more easily by allowing the bow to travel around the string so that each consecutive note is played in a slightly different place on the circumference of the string. With a little experimentation, you will find that the continuing spiraling motion is quite natural. The spiraling loops are clockwise for up-bow staccato and counterclockwise for down-bow staccato.

Part Five

Chapter Eleven
New Left Arm and Hand Alignment

Evolution of the Left Hand Position

In the early part of the 19th century Jean Louis Duport codified the cello technique in his comprehensive work, *Essai sur le Doigte du Violoncelle et la conduite de l'archet, avec une suite d'exercices*. Duport's well-known 21 Etudes are the final chapter of this book.

Duport standardized scale fingerings and established a uniquely cellistic left hand position. He departed from using either the violin or viola da gamba as models.

Duport also established the *extended position,* which is used in the lower half of the cello. In this position, a whole tone between the first and second fingers is played by straightening the first finger. The remaining fingers play only half tones between neighboring fingers. This approach is used by most cellists today.

A New Approach to the Left Arm and Hand

By using a different left arm and hand alignment, it is possible to play whole tones (and even larger intervals at times) with neighboring fingers without stretching. This technique is similar to playing arpeggios on the piano. Playing whole tones with neighboring fingers can be simple, painless, and offers a wealth of new fingering possibilities.

Liberating the Thumb

This new approach is predicated on liberating the thumb from its traditional perch behind the neck of the cello. It allows you to produce a beautiful tone and develop a facile technique without the tension caused by pressing.

When your thumb is free, your arm, forearm and hand are also free. Unrestricted by the traditional thumb placement, you can achieve better balance and reduce tension.

Unlike a violin or viola, the cello does not need to be supported by the left hand or arm. Playing the cello, therefore, does not require constant contact with the thumb. With a liberated thumb, a cellist can traverse the cello as freely as a pianist can move on a keyboard.

Many fine cellists can be observed releasing their thumbs when they vibrate, especially when they are using an extended first finger or playing on the fourth finger. This impulse to release the thumb can also be cultivated with the other fingers.

Placing Fingers With Your Arm

There are no muscles in your fingers. Forearm muscles connected to the tendons in your fingers enable you to move your fingers. Your forearm, in turn, is supported and carried by your upper arm. Your fingers do not naturally move alone, but only as part of the larger complex.

Your fingers can be placed by your entire arm and hand unit with easy, natural, flowing movements. Your arm and all of its parts is an integrated system connected to the rest of your body. When allowed to function together naturally, each body part does the right thing at the right time without tension. When body parts are isolated, tension usually follows.

Placing your fingers with your entire arm-hand unit eliminates excessive and stressful finger movements. This minimizes the danger of overuse injuries frequently associated with finger movements.

More Equal Fingers

Releasing your thumb makes all of your fingers more equal. Cellists typically find their fourth finger weaker than the others. In the traditional position, it is indeed weaker. Your fourth finger, the shortest, receives poorer support from your arm than your other fingers. Liberating your thumb minimizes this disparity. Your arm is able to move freely to support and balance every finger. This also allows you to use your fourth finger more easily in the upper registers.

Vibrato

Removing your thumb from the neck of the cello also makes it easier to maintain a consistent, unwavering vibrato. Vibrato tends to rotate around your thumb when it is held on the neck of the cello. The size of this rotation differs for each finger because each is a different distance from your thumb. When your whole arm is free, your vibrato can flow more evenly and easily from one note to the next.

Chapter Twelve
Exploring the Left Hand and Arm

All of your muscles are more flexible in a released state. Imagine holding the ends of a rubber band between the first finger and thumb of each hand. Stretch and release your imaginary rubber band several times. If you stop flexing but keep the rubber band even partially stretched, it is no longer elastic—it is tense.

Your arm and hand muscles react in much the same way. Your hands are most tension-free when your fingers are in a released state. A left-hand position that keeps your fingers separated requires active muscle power. Opening your hand or straightening a finger is natural and necessary. Yet regularly holding your left hand open with your fingers separated creates unnecessary strain.

To minimize tension, release your hand as much as possible. Open it only as needed. This principle applies to both hands. Holding your fingers too far apart on the bow also creates tension.

Demonstration 26

Thumb and Hand

This demonstration explores the natural impulses of your thumb in relation to the other fingers of your left hand. Perform the breath test with each step.

Step 1. Straighten your fingers and open your left hand.

Step 2. Release your hand, allowing your fingers to come together.

Step 3. Straighten your first finger.

Step 4. Straighten your other fingers one at a time.

Step 5. Straighten any finger, but do not let your thumb move away from your hand.

Step 6. Hold your left hand in the air in your usual playing position.

Step 7. Release your hand as in step two.

Step 8. Move your fingers rapidly.

Step 9. Keep your thumb opposite your second finger and move your fingers rapidly.

Are you more comfortable with your hand open or released?

Do you feel tension when you restrain your thumb as you straighten a finger?

Does your hand feel better in your usual playing position or when it is released?

Which thumb location feels better when you move your fingers rapidly?

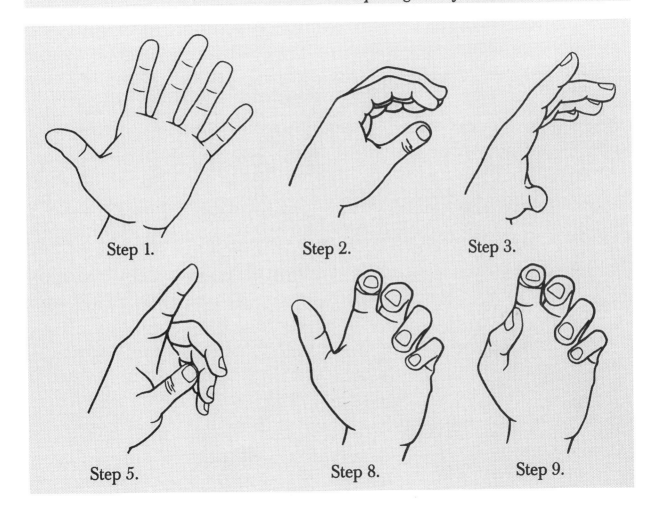

Step 1.

Step 2.

Step 3.

Step 5.

Step 8.

Step 9.

Observations

Your hand and arm are most tension-free when your thumb is allowed to react naturally to the movements of your other fingers. When you straighten your fingers, the natural impulse of your thumb is to move away from your hand. Even when you straighten only one finger, your thumb naturally opens away from your hand. When your fingers move rapidly, the natural impulse of your thumb is to rest alongside your fingers. This can be observed when you play the piano and when you use thumb position on the cello.

Holding your thumb opposite your moving fingers is not a natural impulse. The only time your thumb naturally moves opposite your fingers is when you grasp an object or make a fist. Playing the cello, however, does not require these motions.

Because it is natural for your thumb to move away from your hand when a finger is straightened, restraining it creates tension.

Hand Position

Many students are taught to separate their fingers to keep each finger over a note. Strips of tape are often placed on a beginner's fingerboard to mark finger placements. This does more harm than good. It trains students to hold their fingers tensely apart and to find the notes by using the wrong signals. They are taught to feel for the tape rather than to trust their bodies and their ears. Some are taught to continually press their strings down with as many fingers as possible. These methods make it very difficult to avoid tension.

Demonstration 27

Left Arm and Hand Alignment

This demonstration explores how to find the most comfortable left hand and arm alignment. Observe the alignment of your hand and arm in each step. Perform the breath test with each step.

Step 1. Hold your hand in a released position.

Step 2. With your hand in a released position, raise and lower it slowly to find the most comfortable alignment.

Step 3. Hold your hand in the air and move your fingers rapidly.

Step 4. Move your fingers rapidly, as you raise and lower your hand slowly to find the most comfortable alignment.

Which alignment is most comfortable in a released position?

Which alignment is most comfortable when your fingers are moving rapidly?

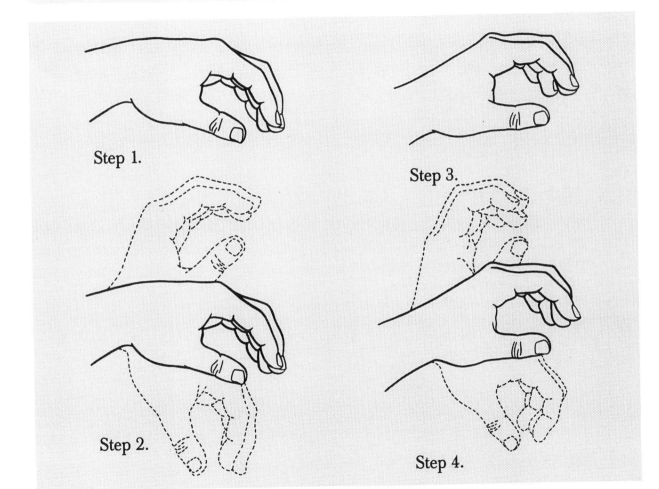

Step 1.

Step 2.

Step 3.

Step 4.

Observations

You are most comfortable when you allow your hand to slant down slightly from your arm in a released position without finger movement. When your fingers are moving you are most comfortable with your hand and arm in a neutral alignment–your hand in line with your arm.

The breath test reveals that no tension is created when your hand and arm are at the most comfortable alignment in each step. It also shows that tension is present when your hand is held too high or too low in relation to your forearm.

Tension-free playing requires that you align your left arm and hand according to how you are using your arm, hand and fingers. The function determines the alignment. Whether you use fingers in a straighter or more curved alignment depends on the combination and speed of notes you are playing at any given moment. One setting cannot accommodate all situations. Awareness of your body's natural impulses can guide you to do the right thing at the right time.

"Too often, players absorbed with the next extension lose sight of the beauty of the note at hand. They widen their fingers in preparation, rather than contracting their hand for a more favorable position for vibrato."
—*Leonard Rose*

Demonstration 28

Path of Fingers

This demonstration illustrates how your fingers can travel when playing the cello. Perform the breath test with each step.

Step 1. With your left hand in the air, move your fingers away from your hand as if you are striking notes on a string.

Step 2. Simulate playing with your fingers moving toward your thumb.

Step 3. Move or wiggle your fingers, allowing them to find their freest path of motion. Allow your arm and forearm to move or rotate freely.

Step 4. Wiggle your fingers without allowing movement in your arm and forearm.

Which finger movements are most comfortable?

Does forearm movement make moving your fingers easier?

Does restricting arm and forearm movement cause tension?

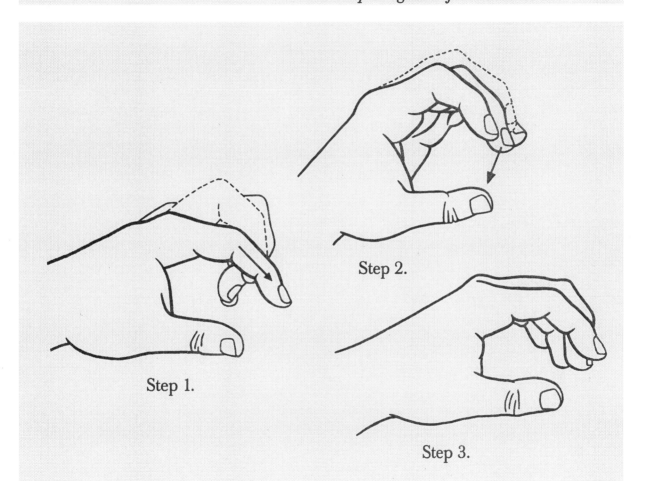

Step 1.

Step 2.

Step 3.

Observations

Moving your fingers away from your hand generates tension. Tension also occurs when your fingers move toward your thumb. When you allow your fingers, arm and forearm to move freely, you are tension-free. The same finger movements are tense, however, when your natural arm and forearm movements are inhibited. This demonstrates that your fingers do not naturally move completely independently. Their movements are integrated with movements of your arm, forearm and hand.

"The difficulty of playing the cello is knowing how to get from one note to the next."
—*Pablo Casals*

Finger Placement

It is widely assumed that the fingers of the left hand must always be placed so that they are centered on their pads. This is logical when the fingers are used to press against the fingerboard or press against the resistance of the thumb.

When pressing is eliminated, however, there are other ways to place your fingers which can make playing easier and offer new technical possibilities.

Demonstration 29

Finger Placement

This demonstration explores left arm, hand and finger placement on the cello.

Step 1. Hold your arm in the air above the cello. Gently bring your arm down and touch the fingerboard on the right side of a string with your first finger. Balance your entire arm and hand unit as you touch with this finger.

Step 2. Allowing your arm and forearm to move freely, gently touch the fingerboard on the right side of a string with your fourth finger. Balance your entire arm and hand unit as you touch with your fourth finger.

Step 3. Play your first, then your fourth finger in your usual playing position.

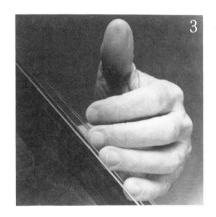

Which part of your finger touches the cello in steps one and two?

Do your arm and forearm move when you go from your first to your fourth finger?

Do you feel more balanced and at ease in steps one and two or in step three?

Observations

When you set your hand or fingers on the cello without turning your forearm inward (pronating), your fingers make contact a bit toward their outside edge. This natural alignment allows greater freedom for your arm and forearm than when pronating to center your fingers. When your entire arm is balanced, your fingers function with their greatest freedom.

Finger movements are integrated with arm and forearm movements. When you move from your first to your fourth finger, you can see and feel your arm moving forward and your forearm rotating.

To touch a string with your first finger, your arm carries your finger toward its destination. When it is within range, your finger automatically drops to the string. As you move to your fourth finger, your first finger is lifted by your arm and rotating forearm as your fourth finger drops to the string.

Chapter Thirteen
Fast and Slow Playing

Fast playing is distinctly different from slow playing and requires a different technique. Fast and slow playing are as different as running and walking. Running is not fast walking nor is walking slow running. In the following sections *slow playing* refers to all except very rapid playing. *Fast playing* refers only to very rapid playing.

Each type of playing uses a different alignment of the left arm and hand. For fast playing, you will be most tension-free if your hand and forearm are in line–in a neutral position. Your fingers also tend to be a bit more rounded for fast than for slow playing. This equalizes their size and allows for a lighter, more facile touch.

Slow playing allows for sufficient time to adjust your arm and hand to the optimum alignment for each finger. Because each finger is a different size and is located in a different place on your hand, a single hand position cannot provide the best balance and support for every finger. If your hand and arm are free, needed adjustments can occur naturally.

Demonstration 30

Fast Playing Action

This demonstration explores finger action in fast playing. Perform the breath test with each step.

Step 1. Simulate fast playing on your right hand by holding as many fingers of your left hand down as you can.

Step 2. Simulate fast playing by tapping the fingers of your left hand downward against your right hand, one at a time.

Step 3. Simulate fast playing by wiggling your fingers in their freest path of motion. Allow your arm to move and let your forearm to rotate to lift your fingers.

Step 4. Move your fingers as in step three but do not let your forearm move.

Step 5. Simulate playing fast notes on the side of a string. Use a finger of your right hand as an imaginary string.

Which steps are the most effortless?

Which interfere with your breathing?

Which allow you to breathe most freely?

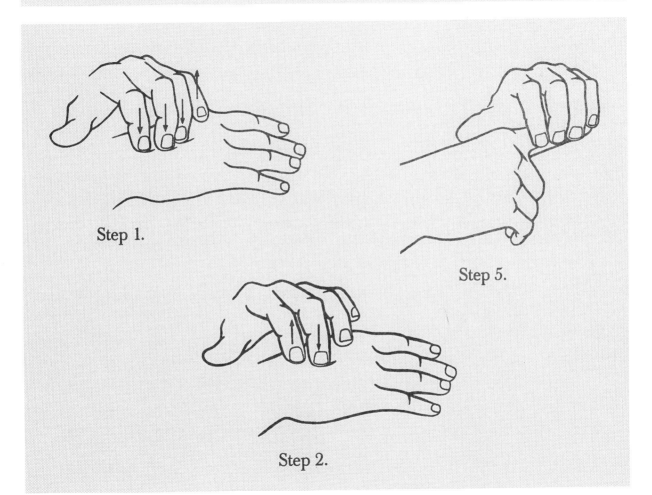

Step 1.

Step 2.

Step 5.

Observations

Many cellists are taught to hold as many fingers down as possible, as in step one. This is the most restrictive way to play and requires considerable muscular effort. Tapping your fingers requires less effort than holding them down but still generates tension. It is easier to move your fingers when your arm and forearm are free to move than when their movements are inhibited. Lifting your fingers with natural forearm motions eliminates tension. This is confirmed by the breath test.

Moving your fingers as if playing on the side of the string requires the least effort of all. This simple and natural sequence of movements is similar to wiggling your fingers. It can be done by anyone and is the basis for the most tension-free fast playing technique. Directing the stroke toward the side of the string provides greater stability and eliminates the impulse to use more force than is needed.

Your fingers touch a soft, springy surface when you play on the side of the string. This is easier than playing percussively against the hard surface of the fingerboard.

As one finger is lifted the next one automatically moves in the opposite direction—toward the string. This naturally-balanced sequence of movement is just like running. When you run, your feet alternately lift and touch the ground. Both feet are never on the ground or in the air at the same time.

Demonstration 31
Fast Playing
This demonstration continues to explore fast playing techniques on the cello.

Step 1. Place your fingers on the wood of the fingerboard between the D and G strings.

Step 2. Play measure one rapidly with your fingers touching the right side of the string as you draw a steady sound with your bow. Allow your left arm and forearm to move freely.

Step 4. Play measure two, keeping your first finger against the string.

Step 5. Play measure two, alternating fingers.

Are you able to produce clear, resonant tones without the string touching the fingerboard?

Do you hear a difference in the rhythmic articulation between alternating fingers and keeping one finger on the string?

Which way sounds more even?

Observations

It may be surprising to discover that good tone production and precision can be achieved at any dynamic level *without the strings touching the fingerboard*. When experiencing this for the first time, some cellists are startled to find out how easy it is. Tones produced in this manner often have greater clarity because the string is never dampened by contact with the fingerboard.

Alternating your fingers in measure two provides more equal articulation on both notes than when one finger remains on the string. This difference is especially apparent when performing mordents or a pair of grace notes. The natural impulse is to alternate rather than to maintain an immobile finger. A finger should only continue touching a string when performing trills.

Elevate Strings

Playing on the side of the strings may be difficult in the lower registers if your strings are too close to the fingerboard. Raising the nut to allow more room between the strings and fingerboard can correct this problem.

It is easy to raise the nut with a temporary strip of wood, or shim. Simply place the wood over the nut beneath the strings. After experimenting to find the most comfortable height, your instrument repair person can install a permanent shim under the nut.

I began my testing with a piece of a popsicle stick and found that I am comfortable with my strings raised about 3/16 of an inch above the fingerboard at the nut.

Slow Playing

How much force, effort or contact with the string is needed to produce clear, resonant tones when playing slowly? Does the string need to be: struck percussively against the fingerboard; pressed firmly against the fingerboard; held lightly against the fingerboard; or held so as not to touch the fingerboard at all?

Surprising as it may seem, a string does not need to touch the fingerboard to produce a clear tone. Very little effort is required to stop the string sufficiently to establish the pitch of a note. A stable point is needed, however, from which to pivot the vibrato. A pivot point is easily established by allowing the end of your finger to rest on the wood of the fingerboard along the right side of the string.

Placing your fingers is done exactly the same way as when you touch an ordinary object. Your arm carries your hand until it is close to the object. When it is within range, your finger drops to touch it. At the same time, your arm balances this finger motion by an impulse to move in the opposite direction. Your finger drops down as your arm lifts. The lift provides the gentle, natural leverage for your hand and finger. Also notice that after you have finished touching an object, your whole arm lifts your finger away. You do not lift your finger independently to remove it.

This is the basis for a tension-free left hand and arm technique. Your finger action is connected to the lifting action of your arm. It does not require pressing or leaning your arm or body weight into the string. When not impeded, this natural sequence of movement occurs automatically. Slow playing this way feels more like caressing the string than striking it.

Demonstration 32

Slow Playing

This demonstration explores a slow playing method which does not require a string to touch the fingerboard.

Step 1. Play the A harmonic on the D string by touching the side of the string with your second finger. Allow your finger to rest on the wood of the fingerboard.

Step 2. Vibrate and draw the string gently to the left until the note drops an octave and you are playing a solid A.

Step 3. Vibrate, pivoting from the wood of the fingerboard. Slowly move your arm up and down and in all directions to find the best balance for your entire arm and hand unit.

Step 4. Play other non-harmonic notes, stopping them in the same way. Play this way with each of your fingers.

Step 5. Try placing the end of your finger different distances from the string as you vibrate at different speeds. See if it is easier to perform a slow, even and steady vibrato with the end of your finger closer or farther from the string.

Step 6. Try playing completely on the right side of the string, especially in the upper registers.

Can you produce a pure, clear tone without the string touching the fingerboard?

Can you vibrate freely this way?

How does this compare to the way you usually play?

Fast playing on side of string

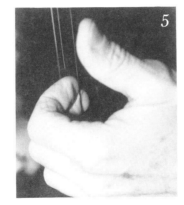

Fast playing

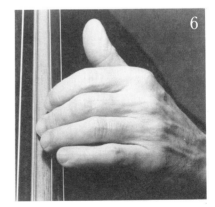

Slow playing

Observations

You can produce a good sound without a string touching the fingerboard. You can, in fact, often produce more resonant and ringing tones when the string does not touch the fingerboard. This is because sound is sometimes dampened when the string touches the wood.

Although a string does not have to touch the fingerboard, it may at times do so. It must never be pressed downward, however, because pressing creates tension.

Each finger is placed by the entire arm and hand unit. Your fingers, as a part of this unit, make only the needed movements with no excessive exertion. Your arm carries your finger to the right place as you change notes and establishes the best balance for each finger.

Placing your fingers with your arm and hand unit is especially important when moving to your fourth finger. Using independent action to stretch a finger away from your hand creates tension. Placing any finger with the entire unit is tension-free. As you play a note on any finger, it should feel as if it is the only finger at the end of your arm.

Some cellists tend to press harder as they play louder. This is a complete waste of energy, because no amount of additional force can increase the volume of sound. When your finger pivots from the wood instead of from the center of the string, the urge to over-press is completely eliminated. Using a lifting action instead of pressing keeps your hand and arm flexible and tension-free.

Pivot Point and Vibrato

Producing a slow, even vibrato is a great challenge for many cellists. Pivoting your vibrato from the wood between strings allows you to easily control the amplitude of your vibrato. The farther your pivot point is from the string, the wider your vibrato will be. Conversely, the closer your finger is to the string, the narrower your vibrato will be.

Place the end of your finger far from the string when you want a slow unwavering vibrato, especially when you play on the lower part of the C string.

Some cellists habitually use an over-intense vibrato when they play on the upper part of the A string. It is easier to moderate your vibrato to produce any degree of intensity you wish by playing on the side of the string with your finger pivoting from the fingerboard.

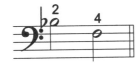

To play a descending fourth, allow your arm to move forward and your forearm to rotate.

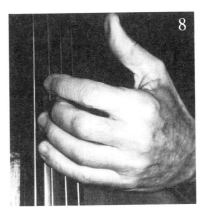

Chapter Fourteen
Shifting

Shifting is a cellist's mode of transportation. It is the way you get from one place to another along the cello fingerboard. Shifts can be performed silently or with deliberate connecting sounds. Ideally, audible sounds should be heard only for artistic reasons. While expressive shifts can enrich a performance, unintended sliding sounds can detract from it.

Although the movements used to shift are different from those used for bowing, there are some similarities. There are two arm levels for shifting just as there are for bowing. An upward shift is performed with the arm at a lower level corresponding to the down-bow level. A downward shift is performed at a higher level, corresponding to the up-bow level.

Although your body's preparatory impulse may be in the direction of the shift, it moves in the opposite direction during the shift. Your body impulse is always in the opposite direction from your shift for the same reason that your bow arm moves opposite to your body impulse—to maintain balance. Steering your body movements with your feet can be as helpful when you shift as when you draw a bow.

All shifting motions are curved. Like bowing, they are always lifted or pulled in response to your body's impulses. They are never pushed.

For cleanly articulated shifts, allow the last finger used before the shift to touch the string and fingerboard lightly throughout the shift. This applies whether a new note is played with the same finger or another. Basic shifting, reduced to its simplest form, *is moving a single finger from one place to another.* The starting finger is your guide to the new location and a new finger is placed only upon arrival at the new note.

Although cleanly articulated shifts are needed most of the time, a variety of audible shifts can be performed by playing a note with one finger and shifting on another, by starting a shift on one finger and switching to another while in motion or by shifting the same finger from one place to another.

Demonstrations 33

Shifting

This demonstration explores the fundamentals of shifting.

Step 1. Play a note with a finger touching the right side of the string and the fingerboard. Rotate your body to the left (in the direction of the shift) to prepare for an upward shift. Your upper arm will move toward the bridge to prepare to pull your hand to a higher note. This is like throwing a ball. Your upper arm precedes your lower arm.

Step 2. Release your hand to shift, rotating your body to the right–in the opposite direction from the shift. Your forearm and hand will spring to the new note as your upper arm moves in the opposite direction–toward the scroll.

Step 3. Play a note with a finger touching the right side of the string and the fingerboard. Lift your arm to a higher level than for an upward shift. Rotate your body to the right. Your upper arm will move toward the scroll to prepare to pull your hand to a lower note.

Step 4. Release your hand to shift and rotate your body to the left. Your hand will spring to the new note. Your upper arm will move in the opposite direction from your forearm–toward the bridge. Keep your arm at the higher level throughout the shift. Release your arm to the lower level only when you arrive at the new note.

Observations

The body movements used for shifting are similar to throwing a ball. Your upper arm is the first part of your arm to move. It is followed by your forearm and hand in that order–from the heavier to the lighter part. This natural sequence occurs when shifting in either direction.

Your body's impulse is always in the opposite direction from your shift. Consciously steering with your feet when you shift is a good way to become accustomed to this total body process.

Preparatory motions are as essential for shifting as for any other body movement. When shifting downward, lifting your arm to the higher level is part of the preparation. When playing rapidly, preparatory motions may only be slight impulses. When playing, slowly, they may be more expansive.

Sliding on the fingerboard with your finger lightly touching the right side of the string minimizes friction. Pressing a string down when you shift is like dragging your foot on the ground when you ride a bicycle.

Reinforcing this concept in the early stages of study builds a secure technical foundation. Once this system is established, shifts can be combined with contractions, expansions (presented in the following chapter) and extensions to shorten the travel distance between notes.

Chapter Fifteen
Expansions, Extensions and Contractions

Expansions

Whole tones, and even larger intervals at times, can be played by neighboring fingers using *expansions*. This term is used to distinguish this technique from the traditional extended position. Expansions are possible only when your arm and forearm can move freely. Your left hand and fingers are carried to each note by your arm with supple and flowing movements

Expansions do not involve stretching. They do, however, require a liberated thumb. When done properly, your arm carries your fingers to their destination with easy, natural movements. The distance between your fingers expands passively. Your fingers are the passengers. Your entire arm and hand unit is the train.

Expansions can add many new options to your repertoire of fingerings. They enable you to connect notes smoothly and securely by eliminating unneeded shifts. They offer new solutions for difficult and awkward passages.

Demonstration 34

Expanding Upward

This demonstration illustrates how to play upward expansions.

Step 1. Play a note with your first finger touching the fingerboard and the right side of a string. Prepare as you would for an upward shift. With a smooth, continuous curve, move your arm forward far enough to carry your second finger a whole tone above your first. As soon as your second finger touches the fingerboard, release your arm and allow your fingers to come together.

Step 2. Play a note with your second finger. Expand in the same manner, placing your third finger a whole tone above your second.

Step 3. Play a note with your third finger in the same way, placing your fourth finger a whole tone above your third. When you move from your third to fourth finger, your arm must travel farther than for other fingers. This is because your fourth finger is so much shorter than your third.

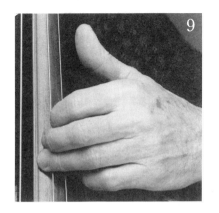

Expand from 3 to 4 by allowing your arm to move forward and your forearm to rotate. Expansions occur passively between the notes. Always close your hand before playing the new note.

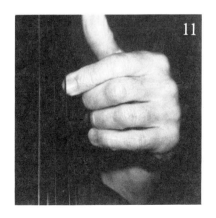

Expand from 1 to 4 by allowing your arm to move forward and your forearm to rotate. Expansions occur passively between the notes. Always close your hand before playing the new note.

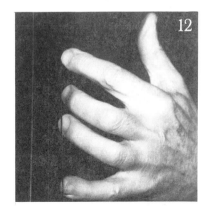

Examples of upward expansions

Saint-Saens Concerto, Second Movement

Beethoven Quartet, Op. 59 #1, First Movement

Saint-Saens Concerto, Third Movement

Dvorak Concerto, Third Movement

Schumann Concerto, First Movement (includes contraction)

E = Expansion   C = Contraction (see page 163)

Demonstration 35
Expanding Downward
This demonstration explores downward expansions.

Step 1. Play a note with your fourth finger touching the fingerboard and the right side of a string. Raise your arm higher for an downward expansion than for an upward one. With a smooth, continuous, clockwise curve, carry your third finger a whole tone below your fourth. Release your hand and arm as soon as your third finger touches the fingerboard.

Step 2. Play a note with your third finger and expand to play a note with your second finger in the same way as in step one.

Step 3. Play a note with your second finger and expand to play a note with your first finger in the same way as in steps one and two.

Examples of downward expansions

Saint-Saens, The Swan

Boccherini Concerto in B flat, Third Movement

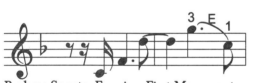

Brahms Sonata, F major, First Movement

Dvorak Concerto, First Movement

Saint-Saens, Concerto, Third Movement (includes upward expansions)

E = Expansion

Demonstration 36

Extended Position

In the standard extended position, the tip of the first finger usually touches the string. This position can be modified at times to make certain note sequences easier to play. This demonstration illustrates an alternate way to use extended position.

Step 1. Play measure one very rapidly, using the traditional extended position.

Step 2. Play measure one rapidly, touching the string closer to the base of your first finger. Try using different parts of your first finger to touch the string. Do not press the string against the fingerboard.

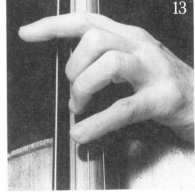

Step 3. Play similar patterns on other strings and in different locations.

Step 4. Play measure two rapidly, using the lower part of your first finger on the upper note of each pair.

Observations

It is sometimes easier to play rapid passages that require an extended position by touching the string closer to the base of your first finger rather than at its tip. The exact placement may vary depending on the note pattern and the size of your hands.

Playing thirds in double stops this way is also easier, particularly when they are in a rapid tempo. It does not really matter which part of your first finger touches the string or which side of a string it touches.

The distance of a whole tone between your first and second fingers is easily spanned when you touch the string closer to the base of your first finger. The traditional extended position can sometimes cause discomfort because the hand is twisted or the wrist is depressed to accommodate the length of the first finger.

Demonstration 37

Contractions

Using contractions to play neighboring notes with non-neighboring fingers is a useful technique that is not new to cellists. Many cellists, however, are either unaware of or neglect this valuable technical option. Contractions are easy to perform and can help make clean, flowing connections between notes by avoiding unnecessary shifts.

The movements needed for contractions are performed by the arm, which carries the fingers to their destinations. This demonstration illustrates how to perform contractions.

Step 1. Play a note with your third finger. Place your first finger next to your third finger by moving your arm toward the bridge and allow your forearm to rotate freely. At the same time, lift your second finger to get it out of the way. Do this as one continuous curved arm movement.

Step 2. Play a note with your fourth finger. Contract to place your second finger next to your fourth finger as you did in step one. Lift your third finger out of the way.

Step 3. Play a note with your fourth finger. Contract to place your first finger on any note between your first and fourth fingers, as you did in step one. Lift your two middle fingers out of the way.

Step 4. Play descending contractions by moving your fourth finger next to your first or second finger or by moving your third finger next to your first finger. Hold your arm at a higher level than for ascending contractions.

Examples of contractions

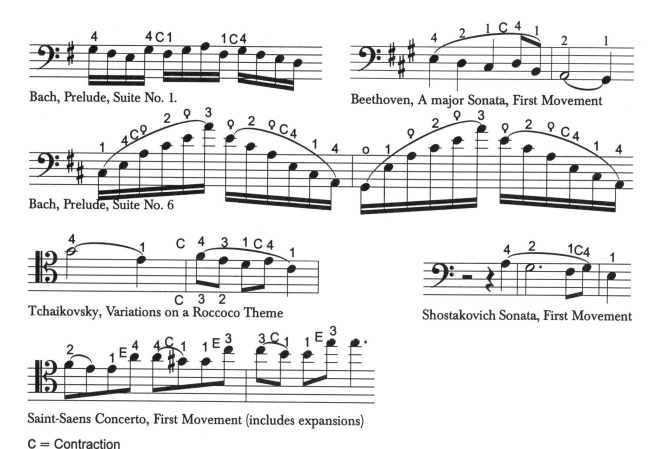

Bach, Prelude, Suite No. 1.

Beethoven, A major Sonata, First Movement

Bach, Prelude, Suite No. 6

Tchaikovsky, Variations on a Roccoco Theme

Shostakovich Sonata, First Movement

Saint-Saens Concerto, First Movement (includes expansions)

C = Contraction

Part Six

Chapter Sixteen
Odds and Ends

Fingerings

Fingering choices are, naturally, influenced by artistic preferences and physical differences. Although there can be no absolute rules about fingering a few general common-sense guidelines are worth considering.

1. Avoid consecutive shifts when possible. They limit preparation time for succeeding shifts and are often in poor musical taste.

2. It is usually better to shift after a longer note than a shorter one. This gives you more time to prepare for the shift.

3. It is often better to shift at bow changes than within slurs.

4. Avoid using the same finger to shift from one string to another location on another string whenever possible. Such shifts tend to be clumsy.

Double Stops and Chords

Balance your entire arm when playing double stops (thirds, fourths, sixths, etc.). When your arm is balanced, your hand and fingers find the right alignment naturally.

Play double stops on the right side of the strings as much as possible. This minimizes tension and frees your vibrato.

Allow your arm and forearm to move freely as you move from note to note. This is especially important when you move to your fourth finger on a lower string. Your fourth finger is shorter than the others. Stretching it to reach away from your hand creates strain. You can even play whole tones between the third and fourth fingers, but only when your arm is positioned correctly and your fourth finger is placed by your arm.

Playing a rapid succession of thirds in the lower part of the cello using the modified extended position, described in Demonstration 36 on pages 161, is a useful option. The point of contact on your first finger can be anywhere from your palm to the tip of your finger, depending on the configuration of notes and the size of your hand. Your first finger can touch the string at the same point for extended or non-extended intervals.

When playing four part chords, it is usually better to place your fingers on notes only as they are needed, rather than holding your fingers on all of the notes at one time. Since four notes cannot be bowed simultaneously, it is not necessary to engage all of your fingers at the beginning of each chord.

The best setting for the lowest note or pair of notes in a four part chord often conflicts with the best setting for the next pair. Playing two notes at a time avoids tension and some of the more awkward positions. It also allows you to vibrate more freely.

Touch the lower note or pair of notes first. Pivot your arm to play the upper notes as your bow approaches the upper strings.

Chords, can often be performed more easily by allowing a finger to reach out beyond the string and to play away from the tip of the finger. This is especially effective when the chord includes fifths that are played with the same finger. Try this in measure one.

Using the same finger to play fifths in measure two is also easier when you play away from the tip of the finger, and with each finger on its outer edge. Playing a bit toward the outer edge of your finger reduces the impulse to press.

It is often better to play the lowest note of a four part chord alone rather than beginning the chord with the lower pair of notes. The tonality of the chord is established more clearly when the root of the chord is heard first. But whether one or two notes are sounded at the beginning of the chord, no more than the required fingers need to be active at the same time.

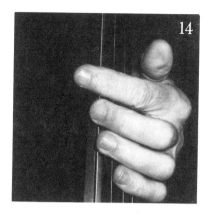

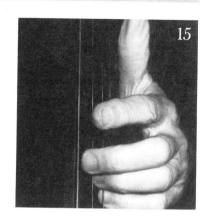

Shifting and Bow Changes

Shift on the old bow stroke to connect shifts cleanly when reversing the direction of your bow. Your bow simply needs to change direction, while your left arm needs to travel some distance before it arrives at the new note. Traveling any distance takes time, whether you go from New York to San Diego or just half an inch. This is why your left arm needs to move before you change the direction of your bow. Your left arm needs a head start to arrive in time to synchronize with the new bow stroke. You can shift on the new bow stroke when you want an audible, expressive slide.

Attention to the speed and character of your bow strokes is essential for good shifting. Shifts are most easily controlled when your bow is moving slowly and at a constant speed.

Connecting Fifths on Neighboring Strings

Fifths on neighboring strings can be connected most smoothly by substituting one finger for another. This simple device avoids any interruption of sound or vibrato.

Saint-Saens, The Swan

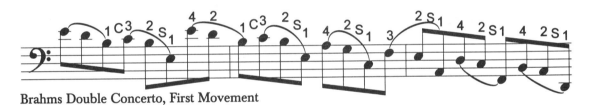

Brahms Double Concerto, First Movement

Brahms, B Major Trio, First Movement

Brahms, B Major Trio, Third Movement

S=Substitution   C=Contraction

Thumb Position

Traditional thumb position places the thumb squarely across two strings, allowing it to function as a movable nut. Liberating the thumb from this role in thumb position provides the same advantage as liberating it in the lower registers.

The only time your thumb must be set squarely across two strings is when you use it to play fifths. Otherwise, it is better to allow your thumb to be free to follow its natural impulse. The only time that your thumb must touch a string is when you use it to play a note.

The position and alignment of your thumb may vary depending on the configuration of the notes you are playing. It is often more convenient to use your thumb on only one string at a time. This is especially so when you play a half tone between your thumb and first finger. At times it is also useful to allow your thumb to contact the string closer to its base than is standard practice. Your other fingers have their greatest flexibility when your thumb is not touching the string at all.

Artificial Harmonics

Although the lower note is usually held down against the fingerboard when playing artificial harmonics, this is not necessary. Harmonics can be played equally well with just a touch contact of both fingers. Eliminating pressing makes harmonics easier to perform.

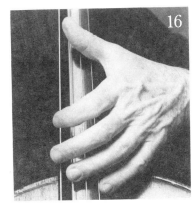

Thumb with deep contact

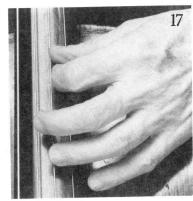

Thumb placed on one string

Trills and Intonation

For perfect intonation, the upper notes of rapid half tone trills must be played flatter than when the same notes are played slowly. Whole tone trills require that the upper note be played sharper than when playing the same note at a slower speed.

These adjustments are necessary because of how the human ear hears rapidly alternating notes. Test this by alternating between two neighboring notes without this adjustment. Trill slowly at first and gradually increase the speed. At some point, the half tone trill begins to sound sharp and the whole tone trill sounds flat.

Direction of Vibrato

Vibrato must always be pulled toward the flat side of a note because the human ear accepts the top of the vibrato's oscillation as the pitch. The first vibrato motion must always lower the pitch.

The upper edge of your finger stops part of the string from vibrating and controls the length of string that is permitted to vibrate. This determines the pitch of each note and holds true whether your finger is as wide as your hand or as thin as a dime.

When vibrato is pulled to the flat side of a note, the body's natural elasticity automatically takes it back to the note. For every pulled stroke you get an extra reactive motion with no additional effort. A vibrato that is pushed upward must be actively returned downward. A pushed vibrato also tends to sharpen pitch and sound tense.

The ideal vibrato expresses the emotion of the music, but is unobtrusive. It is never an entity unto itself. It can vary like the timbre of the human voice. A person sounds quite different when angry than when whispering tender sentiments.

Vibrato is a facet of cello technique that has no threshold of fatigue. In fact, vibrato helps to counteract fatigue and tension. It is much more difficult to hold a long immobile note than a vibrated one.

Chapter 17
Coda

Although this section is titled Coda, it is as much a beginning as an ending. The quest for a better way goes on and on. It is my sincere hope that this book will encourage cellists to explore new ways of playing and stimulate further development of *body-friendly* cello techniques.

Parting Thoughts

Be good to your body. It is the only one you will ever have.

Use a proper seat and place your feet where they can fully support your body. In return, your body will reward you by keeping you free from pain.

If you ignore your body's natural impulses by misaligning it or keeping it immobile, your body will retaliate by making you hurt.

Hold your cello on the left side of your body with your right leg well away from its side. Your bow arm does not like to reach out with no visible means of support.

Lift your body so it can breathe. Don't depress it by pressing.

Keep your body parts sociable and moving together. Don't allow your arm, forearm, wrist or fingers to be soloists. They are happier and more effective as ensemble players.

Always allow your body weight to propel your arms in the opposite direction. Steer with your feet and never lose the connection.

Always use the larger rather than the smaller part of your body. Never ask your arms or muscles to do what your body can do. Never do with a finger what you can do with your arm. Separate your fingers only for good reason.

Liberate your thumb. It will give you untold new freedom in return. Once your thumb is out of bondage you will find a plethora of new fingering possibilities. Your vibrato will be more beautiful than ever and playing will be easier.

Keep your body happy by always moving in curves. Your body does not like to stay on the straight and narrow.

Finally and most importantly, listen to your body and experiment, experiment, experiment.

About the Author

Victor Sazer was born in Kearney, New Jersey in 1926. He studied cello with Leonard Rose at the Juilliard School of Music. He also studied with, Claus Adam, Naum Benditzky, Charles Brennand Sr., Edgar Lustgarten and George Neikrug. His performing career has been wide and varied. After leaving Juilliard, he became a member of the Houston Symphony. He later moved to Los Angeles where he enjoyed an active professional life in the film, television and recording industries and as a chamber musician for many years. He was the cellist of the Coriolan String Quartet, the Viah Trio and the California Chamber Players, among others. Throughout his life, Mr. Sazer has sustained a deep commitment to teaching and is widely recognized for his innovative and creative teaching methods. He served as an artist-teacher of cello and chamber music at the California State University at Long Beach for more than twenty years. Many of his cello students and alumnae of the University String Quartet program, which he founded at Cal-State Long Beach, are now successful professional musicians. As past California State President of the American String Teachers Association (ASTA), he co-founded the highly successful ASTA Summer Institute of Chamber Music. He continues to serve as Artistic Director of the Institute. Mr. Sazer is also a founding board member of the Los Angeles Violoncello Society.